John W Pirsson

The Dutch Grants, Harlem Patents and Tidal Creeks

John W Pirsson

The Dutch Grants, Harlem Patents and Tidal Creeks

ISBN/EAN: 9783337309817

Printed in Europe, USA, Canada, Australia, Japan

Cover: Foto ©ninafisch / pixelio.de

More available books at **www.hansebooks.com**

THE DUTCH GRANTS,

HARLEM PATENTS

AND

TIDAL CREEKS.

THE LAW APPLICABLE TO THOSE SUBJECTS EXAMINED AND
STATED, IN CONNECTION WITH THE TITLES TO

THE McGOWN MARSHES,
(OR THE MEADOWS IN THE BAY OF HELL GATE),
THE HARLEM MILL CREEK,
THE HARLEM MILL POND,
MONTAGNE'S POINT,
MONTAGNE'S FLAT, AND
VAN KEULEN'S HOOK.

With an Appendix,
CONTAINING COPIES OF
ANCIENT DUTCH DEEDS AND RECORDS,
TRANSLATED FROM THE ORIGINALS AND AUTHENTICATED
BY JAMES RIKER, ESQ., AUTHOR OF "HISTORY OF HARLEM,"
AND ALSO, COPIES OF THE HARLEM PATENTS,
AND ILLUSTRATIVE MAP, ETC.

BY
JOHN W. PIRSSON,
Of the New York Bar.

NEW YORK:
L. K. STROUSE & CO., LAW PUBLISHERS,
95 NASSAU STREET.
1889.

PREFACE.

The following pages are the result, in the main, of investigations made by the writer for his own information and for use in his practice. At the suggestion of some of his friends, members of the New York Bar, he ventures to publish this little volume, in the hope that it may be of some service to his brother toilers in the legal profession; especially to those whose attention may not have been particularly turned to the lines of this inquiry.

J. W. P.

NEW YORK, MARCH, 1889.

TABLE OF CONTENTS.

CHAPTER I.

INTRODUCTION.

	PAGE.
The First Ground Brief	1

CHAPTER II.

The Dutch Grants	2

CHAPTER III.

The Indian Titles	9

CHAPTER IV.

The Harlem Patents Interpreted	10

CHAPTER V.

THE FIRST HARLEM FARM.

Montagne's Flat and Montagne's Point	17

CHAPTER VI.

The Village of New Harlem	23

CHAPTER VII.

TIDAL CREEKS.—PART FIRST.

Not all streams in which the tide ebbs and flows are *prima facie* navigable and public.
To raise the presumption that they are public, there must be a public use or navigation.
A private navigation may exist in tidal streams.
The theory that all tidal streams are *prima facie publici juris*, is not sustained by the English Common Law authorities.
The treatise *De Jure Maris*, is probably responsible for that theory, but it does not really teach that doctrine.
The salt marshes and the intersecting creeks are *prima facie* private property.

The common law definition of navigable rivers	32

TABLE OF CONTENTS.

CHAPTER VIII.

TIDAL CREEKS.—PART SECOND.

According to American law, to render a stream public, there must be an actual, or potential, use of water for some useful purpose, connected with trade or agriculture.
The Constitution of the State of New York, of 1777.
The American Authorities as to tidal waters are conflicting and discordant.
English and American Authorities examined and compared.
By the Common law there are three kinds of rivers.
The interpretation of grants bordering on small tidal streams.
No Court of final resort has actually decided, as a matter of law, that all streams in which the tide ebbs and flows, are *prima facie* public and navigable.
The rivulets of Manhattan Island.
The Harlem salt water creeks not public streams.................................. 54

CHAPTER IX.

The McGown Marshes, (or the Meadows in the Bay of Hellgate)....... 85

CHAPTER X.

The Harlem Creek, The Harlem Mill Pond and Van Keulens Hook. Part First.. 107

CHAPTER XI.

The Harlem Creek, The Harlem Mill Pond, and Van Keulen's Hook. Part Second... 124

CHAPTER XII.

Summary.. 128

APPENDIX.

King Charles the Second's Grant of New Netherland, &c., to the Duke of York... 130
The Duke of York's Commission to Colonel Richard Nicolls............. 135
Agreement between John Montagne and John Louwe Bogert for the sale of Montagne's Point, or Rechawanes, and the Meadows in the Bay of Hell Gate.. 137
Deed from the Magistrates of Harlem to John Montagne for Montagne's Point and the Meadows in the Bay of Hell Gate............ 138

TABLE OF CONTENTS. VII

Deed from Mrs. Maria Vermilje, the widow of John Montagne, to John Louwe Bogert, for Montagne's Point and the Meadows in the Bay of Hell Gate.. 146

Resolution of the Constable and Magistrates, estimating the land of Bogert purchased from Lamontagne at 18 *morgen*...................... 139

Deed for the Hop Garden by Maria Vermilje, widow of Jan de Lamontagne, to Cornelia Everts, wife of Jan Louwe van Schoonrewoert (or Bogert).. 140

Judgment in Joost Von Oblinus *v.* Jan Louwe Bogert, relating to a small meadow in the southerly end of the Bay of Hell Gate...... 141

Deed of the Overseers and Authorized Men of Harlem, to Jan Louwe Bogert, for a piece of land lying in the Bend of Hell Gate. Being Lot No. 25 of common lands.. 142

Deed of the Overseers and Authorized Men of Harlem, to Jan de Lamaeter, for a piece of land lying in the Bend of Hell Gate. Being Lot No. 26 of common lands...................................... 143

Minutes of the Town of Harlem, dated Jan'y 3d, 1667, relative to building the dam for Delavall's Mill at Harlem Creek............. 145

Historical statement of James Riker, Esq., relative to lots Nos. 21, 22, 23 and other lots on Van Keulen's Hook, and Jochem Pieter's tract, &c... 147

Minutes of the Town of Harlem of Oct. 23d, 1738, containing grant to Samson Benson to build a dam and a mill on the Mill Camp " in place of Delavall's Mill gone to decay,"............................. 150

Award of Lewis Morris of the Manor of Morrisania, Abraham Van Wyck and others, on behalf of the freeholders of the township of New Harlem, alloting the Mill Camp Tract adjoining the Mill Pond, to Benjamin Benson.. 151

Certificate of James Riker, Esq., author of the History of Harlem, authenticating Dutch documents... 154

Patent of Richard Nicolls, Governor, &c., to the Freeholders and Inhabitants of Harlem, of 1666... 156

Patent of Richard Nicolls, Governor, &c., to the same, 1667............. 159

Patent of Thomas Dongan to the same, of March, 1686................... 162

Opinion of Richard O'Gorman, Esq., Counsel to the Corporation of New York... 167

Opinion of William C. Whitney, Esq., Counsel to the Corporation of New York... 170

Opinion of the Hon. Murray Hoffman, relating to Harlem Mill Creek. 174

Second Avenue Opening—Extracts from Report of Commissioners.... 181

Extracts from proceedings for opening 106th and 107th Streets, with Map... 185

Illustrative Map.. 187

INDEX TO TABLE OF CASES CITED.

Atkinson v. Bowman (5 N. Y. State Reporter)..................13, 15
Breen v. Lock (N. Y. State Reporter)............13, 63, 74, 75, 76
Bristow v. Cornican (3 App. Cases, House of Lords)....49, 104
Buck v. Squires (22 Vt)........... 117
Canal Commissioners v. Kempshal (26 Wend.).................. 54
Canal Commissioners v. The People (5 Wend. S. C. 17 Wend.)......................6, 7, 55
Child v. Starr (4 Hill).....59, 70, 117
Commonwealth v. Charlestown (1 Pick. Mass. R.)..........56,65
Culver v. Rhodes (87 N. Y.)..... 100
Denton v. Jackson, or Town of Hempstead (2 Johnson Ch. R.)......................13, 14, 15
Elder v. Burras (6 Humph. Tenn. R.)...................... 60
Ex parte Jennings (6 Cow.).5, 7, 64
Ex parte Tibbets (5 Wend.)..... 59
Florence v. Hopkins, (46 N. Y.) 99, 100
Johnson v. McIntosh (8 Wheaton, U. S. R.)................... 5, 9
Luce v. Carley (24 Wend.)...... 116
Martin v. Waddell (16 Peters, U. S. R.)...................... 5
Mayor of N. Y. v. Hart (95 N. Y. S. C. 16 Hun). 7, 13, 15, 69, 74, 76
Mayor of Lynn v. Turner (1 Cowper)..45, 52, 55, 64, 80, 81, 83
Mayor etc., Colchester v. Brook (7 Queens Bench)...........47, 67
McCannon & others v. Sinclair & others (Ellis & Ellis., Rep.). 48
McManus v. Carmichael (2 Clark Cases, Iowa R.).......... 60

New York & Brooklyn Saw Mill & Lumber Co. v. The City of Brooklyn (71 N. Y.)..52
Ogden v. Lee (6 Hill).......... 9
People v. The Canal Appraisers (33 N. Y.).............63, 74, 78
People v. Allen (42 N. Y.)....... 53
Providence Steam Engine Co. v. Providence (12 Rhode Island R.)......................65, 83
Rex v. Montague (4 Barnwell and Cresswell R.), 41, 65, 79, 81, 83
Rex v. The Inhabitants of Landulph (1 Moody & Robinson's) 48
Roberts v. Baumgarten (51 N. Y. Supr. Ct. and S. C. 110 N. Y.).54, 72, 76, 77, 81, 82, 111, 117
Rodgers v. Jones (1 Wend.)...... 13, 55, 69, 117
Royal Fishery of Banne. 49
Seneca Nation v. Knight (23 N. Y.)............................ 116
The Montillo (20 Wall. U. S. Rep.)........................... 67
The Daniel Ball (10 Wall. U. S. R.)......................... 67
Trustees of East Hampton v. Kirk (68 N. Y.)................... 15
Trustees of Duke of Bridgewater v. Highways of Bootle (7 Best & Smith & S. C. 2 Law R. 2 B. 4)............48, 65
Vooght v. Winch (2 Barnwell & Alderson's R.)...........47, 82
Rowe et al v. The Granite Bridge Co.(21 Pick. Mass. R.) 38, 62, 65
Williams v. Wilcox '(8 Ad. & El.)........................... 48

CHAPTER I

INTRODUCTION.

The First Ground Brief.

It is not generally known that the two historic tracts of land, Montagne's Point and Montagne's Flat, originally formed but one Bouwery or farm, and that subsequently they were divided, and the "Meadows in the Bay of Hellgate" were added to Montagne's Point farm. The territory thus united continued under one title until it came to be possessed by Margaret McGown, in 1821, by inheritance from her father, Samson Benson, who was a lineal descendant of Johannes Benson, the first grantee of record whose deed from Jan Loussen Bogert bears date in 1706.

The title to Montagne's Flat and Montagne's Point had its beginning in the first ground brief granted by the Dutch government of any part of Harlem, and probably of any part of Manhattan Island.

Van Keulen's Hook ranks next in antiquity.

"Muscoota," The Flat, was the euphonious name of the Harlem Plains conferred by the Indians; and "Rechawanes," or Great Sands, the unmistakably Indian designation for the neck or point of land lying between Harlem creek and the creek at the south leading through the meadows in the bay between Rechawanes and Hoorn's Hook. In fact, the title to the Point farm from the first included more than half of those meadows.

CHAPTER II.

The Dutch Grants.

Before going into the history of these ancient farms, Montague's Flat and Montague's Point, with the adjoining meadows and intersecting creeks, the preliminary question naturally arises as to the beginning of land titles on Manhattan Island.

To whom did the territory originally belong? Was it, under the law of nations, vested in the British Crown by virtue of the voyages and discoveries of Cabot in 1498, and the subsequent voyages of Gilbert, Sir Walter Raleigh and other British subjects? Or was it vested in the Dutch government, through the visit of Hendrick Hudson in September, 1609, to the Bay of New York, and his subsequent explorations of the Hudson? This is more than an interesting historical inquiry; it has a bearing on the question as to the law applicable to the interpretation of the grants and property rights resting upon Dutch authority.

A brief statement of the case will not, therefore, be inappropriate.

The fact that the British Crown had periodically laid claim to the territory of New Netherland, founded upon the discoveries of Cabot and of other navigators sailing under the British flag and authority, and the claim that the Dutch were mere intruders, was the justification alleged for the advent of the English fleet and forces under Nicolls at New Amsterdam, in the time of profound peace with Holland.

That the British were confident of the validity of their claim is shown by the fact that the patent for the territory of New Netherland by Charles the Second, to the Duke of York, was granted before the armament sailed, as was also the commission of the duke to Nicolls.

(See the patent and commission, Appendix A.)

The seizure of the New Netherland by the British forces, and their occupation of the territory in 1664, practically settled the controversy for the time, and the relinquishment of it by the Dutch in the treaty of Westminster in 1674, removed all doubt as to the ultimate title in the English. The treaties of surrender in 1664 and 1674 having preserved the *statu quo* of the inhabitants, no disturbance was made of vested rights in private persons.

In regard to the forcible entry of the British, Brodhead says (History of the State of New York, vol. 1., p. 745):

"The reduction of New Netherland was now accomplished. The flag of England was at length triumphantly displayed, where, for half a century, that of Holland had rightfully waved, and from Virginia to Canada, the King of Great Britain was acknowledged as sovereign . . . . . but whatever may have been its ultimate consequences this treacherous and violent seizure of the territory and possessions of an unsuspecting ally, was no less a breach of private justice than of public faith."

The brief re-occupation of the Dutch under Governor Clove, extending from August, 1673, to November, 1674, raised serious doubt as to the title of the Duke of York. In regard to this, Brodhead says in his history (Vol. 2, p. 260):

"By the Treaty of Westminster the United Provinces relinquished their conquest of New Netherland to the King of England. The sovereign States General had treated directly with Charles as sovereign. A question at once arose at Whitehall about the subordinate interest of the Duke of York. It was claimed by some that James' former American proprietorship was revived.

"Yet, while the treaty of Westminster re-established the Articles of Capitulation agreed to by Nicolls and Stuyvesant, who represented their sovereigns in 1664, it did not cure the imperfections subject to which the Duke had for nine years governed his American provinces. James's patent had been sealed while the Dutch were in quiet possession of New Netherland, and no new grant was made to him after the Treaty of Breda, which confirmed to the English King his conquest of the Dutch provinces. Eminent lawyers 'very justly questioned' the Duke's pretension to the territory which England had recently recovered; because its cession to her sovereign by the Dutch government had given no strength to original defects. James was now obliged to give up the claim as of English right which he and his brother had formerly maintained. The opinion of counsel having been taken, they advised that the Duke's proprietorship had been extinguished by the Dutch conquest, and that the king was now alone seized of New Netherland, by virtue of the Treaty of Westminster. The *jus postliminii* did not obtain in New York.

"A new patent to the Duke of York was therefore sealed. By it the king again conveyed to his brother the territories he had held before, and granted him anew the absolute powers of government he had formerly enjoyed over British subjects, with like additional authority over 'any other persons' inhabiting his province."

The second patent was identical with the first.

"To quiet any controversy about the *jus postliminii*, Andros issued a proclamation on November 9th, 1674, that all former grants, privileges, or concessions heretofore granted, and all estates legally possessed by any under His Royal Highness, before the late Dutch government, as also all legal judicial proceedings during that government, prior to my arrival by these parts, are hereby confirmed, and the possessors by virtue thereof to remain in quiet possession of their rights. It is hereby further declared that the known Book of Laws formerly established and in force under His Royal Highness's government, is now again confirmed by His Royal Highness, the which are to be observed and practiced, together with the time and manner of holding Courts therein mentioned as heretofore." (Brodhead Id. Vol. 2, p. 273).

On this subject Hoffman says (Estates of N. Y. p. 92):

"It can not be questioned at this day, that the right of discovery and occupation of New Netherland, and particularly of Manhattan Island was in the Dutch, and that the claims of the English were unfounded." As this opinion appears to rest entirely upon Brodhead as its authority, it does not add much weight to that side of the controversy.

On the other hand, we have among others, these adverse authorities: "From the time of the settlement, the English claimed New Netherland as part of Virginia, resting their claim upon the discovery of Cabot. In 1622 the English minister at the Hague demanded the abandonment of the Dutch settlements on the Hudson. Five years afterwards, Governor Bradford, of Plymouth, gave notice to Governor Minuit that the patent of New England covered the domain of New Netherland." (Lossing's Encyclopædia of U. S. History, New York, Harper, 1881. Vol. 2, p. 997).

"The States of Holland also made acquisitions in America, and sustained their right on the common principle adopted by all Europe. . . . The claim of the Dutch was always contested by the English, not because they questioned the title given by discovery, but because they insisted on being themselves the rightful claimants under that title. Their pretensions were finally settled by the sword." (Marshall, Ch. J., in Johnson v. McIntosh, 8 Wheaton U. S. R., p. 574).

"The country granted by King Charles II. to the Duke of York, was held by the King in his public and regal character, as the representative of the nation and in trust for them. The discoveries made by persons acting under authority of the government, were for the benefit of the nation; and the Crown according to the British constitution was the proper organ to dispose of the public domain." (Johnson v. McIntosh, Id., p. 598).

In Martin v. Waddell, (16 Peters, U. S. Rep., p. 403,) Taney, Ch. J., in delivering the opinion of the Court, says: "The right of the King to make this grant, with all its prerogatives and powers of government, cannot, at this day, be questioned. But in order to enable us to determine the nature and extent of the interest which it conveyed to the Duke, it is proper to inquire into the character of the right claimed by the British Crown, *in the country discovered by its subjects, on this continent*, and the principles upon which it was parcelled out and granted.

"The English possessions in America *were not claimed by right of conquest, but by right of discovery*. For according to the principles of international law as understood by the then civilized powers of Europe, the absolute rights of property and dominion were held to belong to the European nation by which any particular portion of the country was first discovered." pp. 408 and 409.

"*The grant to the Duke of York, therefore, was not of land won by the sword; nor were the government or laws he was authorized to establish intended for a conquered people.* The country mentioned in the letters patent was held by the King in his public and regal character, as the representative of the nation and in trust for them." p. 409.

"It (the letters patent) was an instrument on which was to be founded the institutions of a great political community; and in that light it should be regarded and construed. They (the letters patent) were made for the purpose of enabling the Duke of York to establish a colony upon the newly discovered continent to be governed, as nearly as circumstances would permit, *according to the laws and usages of England*." p. 412.

In Canal Commissioners v. The People, (5 Wendell, p. 445,) Walworth, Chancellor, says: "On these principles it is contended that as the State was orginally settled by a colony of the Dutch, the rule of the *civil law* prevails as to all of our streams which are navigable with boats or rafts above tide water. Or at least, that the rule of the common law on this subject was local; was wholly inapplicable to the fresh water rivers of this State, and for that reason, was never in force in the colony.

"There might be some weight in the first of these objections if the crown of Great Britain, or the colonial government had ever claimed this province by right of *conquest*. But it is a matter of history, that it was always claimed by right *of discovery, and not as a conquered country, and that no part of the civil law, as such*, except that which was derived from England, has ever been in force in this colony. The recitals in the patent under which the relator claims title, show that the province was granted to the Duke of York, as part of the domain of the crown, several months before the surrender to Sir Richard Nicolls and before any attempt had been made to take possession thereof by force. The guaranty to the Dutch settlers of the peaceable enjoyment of their possessions did not alter the British claim to the country."

In the same case, (17 Wendell p. 587,) the Chancellor further enforces the same doctrine. He says: "By the charter to the Duke of York of March 1664, under the great seal of England, it is declared in express terms that the laws to be established in the province, shall not be contrary to, but as near as may be agreeable to the laws and statutes and government of England. This charter therefore, was in itself an explicit declaration of the King's will that the laws of England should be established in this colony; *and absolutely deprived the Duke of the power of retaining the laws of the ancient Dutch settlers*, and thereby the Laws of England then in force *ipso facto* became those of the colony, immediately upon the surrender of the Dutch to Governor Nicolls in August of the same year."

Finch, J. in Mayor v. Hart, 95 N. Y. 450, in delivering the opinion of the Court, says: "Two years earlier the Dutch surrendered New Amsterdam to Colonel Nicolls, who with an armed force, asserted the right and authority of the Duke of York and English government. The common law of England entered the City with him."

Mr. Gould in his admirable treatise on the Law of Waters, and Riparian Rights, says, p. 67: "In territories acquired by discovery, the rights of the new settlers are determined by the laws of the mother country, which become immediately applicable; but in lands acquired by conquest, the conqueror may prescribe what law he pleases. The early English settlements in this country, upon the Atlantic coast, were of the former class, the lands which were occupied by the colonists being claimed by the crown of England by right of discovery. A grant from the king could alone confer title to the soil, and was the only source of authority for exercising the powers of government over the lands so granted. The absolute right of property and dominion was thus held to belong to the European nation by which any particular portion of the country was first discovered, as if it had been without inhabitants. . . . . . In New York, which was settled by the Dutch, with whom the civil law prevailed, the province was claimed by right of discovery, when it passed into the possession of the English, and being re-established as a British colony, the common law of England was applied in controversies respecting its waters."

By the constitution of the State of New York of 1777, it is declared "that such parts of the common law of England and of the statute law of Great Britain and the acts of the legislature of the colony of New York, as together did form the laws of the colony on the 19th day of April, 1775, should be and continue the Laws of this State."

These authorities show conclusively that the Dutch never had any right to New Netherland; that the title of Great Britain was absolute and indisputable. They further show in the words of Chancellor Walworth, "*that no part of the civil law, as such, except that which was derived from England, has ever been in force in this colony.*" And it follows that all questions arising out of grants and interests in real property, derived under the Dutch government, must be construed and determined by the laws of England, as they existed prior to the American revolution.

There is no authoritative statement of just what the Roman Dutch law was, to what extent it embodied the civil law, or in what respects it differed from the common law.

CHAPTER III.

The Indian Titles.

As to these the doctrine as recognized by the Supreme Court of the United States is, that the titles and right to possession in America were by discovery, and that the Indian tribes were regarded as temporary occupants of the soil; that this doctrine was as applicable to the Dutch Government as to the English sovereign. (8 Wheaton 595, 16 Peters 367, *supra*.)

The sovereignty and ultimate title was in the European nation, which made the discovery, but the immediate right of possession was in the Indians. The claims set up and asserted amounted to little more than a pre-emption, or right of purchasing from the Indians, all the lands within the bounds of their respective discoveries, to the exclusion of other nations.

The charter and patents for lands in this State, before the Indian titles were extinguished, gave only the ultimate fee or right of dominion after such extinguishment. The title of the Indians by occupation has been uniformly acknowledged both by the Colonial and State Governments.

Pr. Bronson, Justice, Ogden v. *Lee,* 6 Hill, p. 548.

The occupation of Manhattan Island by the Dutch, prior to the appointment of Peter Minuit, the first Governor, in 1624, was merely by sufferance, but it was then determined to make a permanent settlement thereupon. Accordingly one of the first acts of the Director, after his arrival at New Amsterdam, was to purchase from the Indians the Island of Manhattan, which he did in the year 1626, for the sum of sixty guilders. The Island was supposed to contain about twenty-two thousand acres.

The Dutch Government thus united in itself the entire estate in accordance with the rules above laid down. "The Director-General was absolute, as representing the sovereign authority. He extinguished Indian title to land, sanctioned all purchases from the aborigines, erected Courts, made laws, issued ordinances, granted lands, incorporated towns, imposed taxes, and acted in a judicial capacity."

O'Callaghan History of New Netherlands, Vol. 1, pp. 89, 90, 100.

At the time of the British entry in 1664, the Village of of New Harlem was a flourishing settlement. It was a Town in fact, although it is probable that no formal charter had been granted. The first Nicolls' Patent, speaks of it as a "town and lands thereto belonging." Two subsequent confirmations were given. These will now be considered.

CHAPTER IV.

The Harlem Patents Interpreted.

The first and original Harlem Patent was granted by Governor Nicolls in May, 1666. The caption of this patent as recorded in the Office of the Secretary of State, reads : "A Patent granted unto the Freeholders and Inhabitants of Harlem, alias Lancaster, upon the Island of Manhattan."

The patent recites that : "Whereas there is a certain Town or Village commonly called or known by the name of New Harlem, ... now in the tenure or occupation of several freeholders and inhabitants, who have been at considerable charge in building as well as manuring, planting, fencing the said town and lands thereunto belonging. Now for a confirmation unto the said freeholders and inhabitants in their enjoyment and possession of their particular lots and estates, in said town, and also for the encouragement to them in the further improvement of the said lands, . . . I have thought fit to ratify, confirm and grant, and by these presents do ratify, confirm and *grant unto the said freeholders and inhabitants*, their heirs, *successors* and assigns, and to each and every of them *their particular lots and estates*, in the said Town, or any part thereof; and *I do like-*

wise confirm and grant unto the freeholders and inhabitants in general, their heirs, *successors*, and assigns, *the privileges of a Town;* but immediately depending on this City, as being within the liberties thereof. Moreover for the better ascertaining of the *lands to the said Town belonging*, the extent of their bounds shall be as follows, viz.: That from the west side of the fence of the said Town, a line run due west four hundred English poles without variation of the compass, at the end whereof another line being drawn to North and South with the variation, that is to say, North to the very end of a certain meadow ground, commonly called the Round Meadow, near or adjoining to Hudson River, and South to the Saw Mills, over against Hoog Island, commonly called Ferkins Island. It shall be the West bounds of their lands, and all the lands lying, being within the said line, so drawn North and South, as aforesaid, eastward to the town and Harlem River, as also the North and East Rivers shall belong to the said town. Together with all the soils, creeks, quarries, woods, meadows, pastures, marshes, waters, fishing, hunting and fowling. And all other profits, commodities, emoluments and hereditaments to the lands and premises within the said line belonging, or in any wise appertaining with their and every of their appurtenances; *to have and to hold*, all and singular, the said lands, hereditaments and premises, with their and every of their appurtenances, and of every part and parcel thereof, *to the said freeholders* and inhabitants, their heirs, *successors*, and assigns, *to the proper use and behoof of the said freeholders and inhabitants*, their heirs, *successors* and assigns forever.

"It is likewise further confirmed and granted, that the inhabitants of the said Town shall have liberty, for the conveniency of more range of their horses and cattle, to go farther west into the woods, beyond the aforesaid bounds, as they shall have occasion, the lands lying within being intended for plowing, home pasture and meadow grounds only; and no person shall be permitted to build any manner of house or houses within two miles of the aforesaid limits or bounds of the said town, without the consent of the inhabitants thereof. *And the said freeholders and inhabitants of the said Town*, are to observe and keep the terms and conditions hereafter expressed, that is to say: That from and after the date of these presents the said Town shall no longer be called New Harlem, but shall be known and called by the name of Lancaster. . . . . And the *freeholders and inhabitants*, their heirs, *successors* and assigns, are likewise to render and pay all such acknowledgments and duties as already are or hereafter shall be constituted and ordained by his Royal Highness, the Duke of York, and his heirs, or such Governor and Governors as shall from to time be appointed and set over them. Given under my hand and seal, at Fort James, in New York on Manhattan Island, the   day of May, in the eighteenth year of the reign of our sovereign Lord Charles the Second, by the grace of God, King of England, Scotland, France and Ireland, Defender of the Faith, &c., and in the year of our Lord God, 1666.

"RICHARD NICHOLLS."

The Patent first confirms and grants unto the " said freeholders and inhabitants the enjoyment and possession of their particular lots and estates in the said town, and it likewise confirms and grants unto the *freeholders and inhabitants in general*, their heirs, *successors* and assigns *the privileges of a town*, but immediately depending upon this City, as being within the limits thereof, and that for the better ascertaining of the limits of the said *lands to the said Town belonging*, the extent of their bounds shall be as follows, &c. To have and to hold, all and singular the said lands, hereditaments, and premises, with their appurtenances, unto the said *freeholders and inhabitants*, their heirs, *successors* and assigns forever."

The grant was made to the *freeholders and inhabitants as a community*, and to their *successors*. The patent constituted them a corporation. The unappropriated or *common lands*, by this charter became invested in the community, the freeholders and inhabitants in their corporate capacity, in trust for said town.

Denton v. *Jackson* (*or Hempstead, town of*) 2 Johnson,
Cy., R., p. 324–327.
The Mayor, &c. v. *Hart,* 16 Hun, p. 381, and
Same case, 95 N. Y., p. 450.
Atkinson v. *Bowman,* Gen. T., 2d Dist., N. Y. State,
Rep., Vol. 5, p. 456.
Rogers v. *Jones,* 1 Wend., 238.
Breen v. *Locke,* N. Y. S. R., Vol. 11, p. 288.

The patent granted by Governor Nicolls in 1667 was not a new patent, but a confirmation of the first, and intended to make that patent more definite and certain as to the limits and description of the land granted, and to restore the name of New Harlem to the town in place of Lancaster, which was unacceptable to the inhabitants.

The Mayor, &c., v. *Hart,* 16 Hun, 382; Riker's History, p. 265; Riker's Hist. of Harlem, 255.

In this case, Judge Daniels says: "These patents were made and delivered in May 1666, and October 1667, for that which followed them in 1686 (meaning the Dongan patent) was merely confirmatory of the preceding grants. By these two prior patents the lands described and the privileges mentioned in them were given and granted to the freeholders and inhabitants of what is stated at that time became the town or village of New Harlem." The grants made by these patents were not to individuals, but to the town or village whose prosperity and growth had attracted the attention of the colonial governor. The dates in this report are erroneously printed October, 1666, instead of 1667, and 1668, instead of 1686.

In Breen *v.* Locke, id. p. 380, the Court holds that the "*Nicolls patents granted to the freeholders of Harlem* a tract of land bounded," etc., and on page 391: "Our conclusion that the land in question was conveyed to the *freeholders and inhabitants* by the patents already mentioned." See also the act of the legislature of March 28, 1820, chapter 115, providing for the appointment of trustees of the freeholders and inhabitants of Harlem, relative to the sale of the Harlem Commons.

The confirmatory patent of Governor Nicolls adds to the description: The island is called "Vercher's or Hogg Island, in the Sound or East river," and after the words Harlem river is added, "or any part of the said river on which this island doth abut"; and also . . . "*doth and shall belong to the said Town.*" Also "four lots of meadow ground upon the main, marked with the numbers 1, 2, 3, 4, over against the Spring," . . . "With a small island commonly called Stony Island, lying to the East of the Town and Harlem River, going through Bronk's Kill, by the Little and Great Barne's Islands, upon which there are four other lots of meadow ground marked with Nos. 1, 2, 3, 4."

This confirmation patent recites that the village or town commonly called New Harlem is in the tenure or occupation of several of the *freeholders and inhabitants, settled there by authority,* and that there are also settled thereupon *a competent number of families, capable to make a township,* and that for a *confirmation to the said freeholders and inhabitants* in their possession and enjoyment of the premises, *and also for the further improvement of the said lands it ratifies, confirms* and grants unto Thomas Delavall, Esq., John Verveelen, Daniel Tourneur, Joost Oblinus, and Resolved Waldron, as patentees, for and on behalf of themselves and their associates, the freeholders and inhabitants of the said town, their heirs, successors and assigns, all that tract, etc. The *habendum* is to the patentees, and their associates and successors.

The associates of the five patentees named in this confirmation patent meant the freeholders and inhabitants at large.

Denton v. *Jackson, supra,* p. 326.

The individuals named in this patent were created a Board of Trustees for the *freeholders and inhabitants* and commonalty of the town, and their successors. The grant was one to the freeholders and inhabitants of the town, and it was to be in trust for the freeholders and inhabitants.

Atkinson v. *Bowman*, N. Y. State Reporter, v. 5, p. 47.
Trustees of Easthampton v. *Kirk*, 68 N. Y. p. 459; same case, 84 N. Y. p. 261.

The word *heirs* in the grant refers to the estates which the freeholders and inhabitants held at that time in severalty, as their respective individual property. The word *successors* refers to the lands, which by the charter were granted to the freeholders and inhabitants in common, for the uses of the township. The word successors is a well-known technical term applied to corporate succession, and it coupled with the grant of the lands all the privileges and immunities belonging to a town. Both parties had the same object in view, the town which applied and the government which granted.

Denton v. *Jackson*, *supra*, p. 327.

The Dongan patent of March, 1686, was simply a confirmation and ratification of the rights granted under the original Nicolls patent.

Mayor, etc., v. *Hart*, 16 Hun, pp. 381–4.

It begins by reciting that: "Whereas Richard Nicolls, Esquire, formerly Governor of this province, by his writing or Patent bearing date the eleventh day of October, 1667, did give, ratify, confirm and grant unto Thomas Delavall, Esq., John Verveelen, Daniel Tourneur, Joost Oblinus and Resolved Waldron, as Patentees for and on behalf of themselves and their associates, the freeholders and inhabitants of New Harlem, their heirs, *successors* and assigns, all that tract, etc., to have and to hold, unto the said patentees and their associates, their successors and assigns, etc. Whereas the present inhabitants and freeholders of the Town of New Harlem aforesaid have made their application unto me, for a more full and ample confirmation of their premises to them, their heirs, successors and assigns forever, in their quiet and peaceable possession;" and it further recites, "that whereas Richard Nicolls, Esq., did ratify, confirm and grant unto the said patentees and their associates, and their successors and assigns, all the rights and privileges belonging to a town," . . . . "Now know ye, that in consideration of the premises, and of the Quit Rents hereinafter reserved, I have given, granted, ratified and confirmed, and by these presents do give, grant, ratify and confirm unto John Delavall, etc. (naming 23 in all), as patentees, for and on behalf of themselves, the present freeholders and inhabitants of the Town of New Harlem, their heirs, successors and assigns." It amplifies the description in the grant by adding the words, "messuages, tenements, houses, buildings, barnes, stables, orchards, gardens, pastures, mills, *mill-dam*, *runs*, *streams*, ponds, underwoods, trees, timber, fencings, liberties and privileges." The "Round Meadows" near or adjoining unto the "Hudson's River," mentioned in the patent, was a parcel of salt meadow near the foot of 129th Street. The insertion of the names of twenty-three individuals in the patent, in lieu of the five in the second Nicolls patent, was simply an enlargement of the Board of Trustees or representatives of the town; *the patent was in confirmation of the rights already granted and vested*. (See cases above cited.)

The original patent of Nicolls conferred the grants and established the rights of the patentees; the two subsequent patents show clearly and conclusively that they were merely confirmatory, and that the persons named therein took no interest or estate in the common lands granted, in their individual capacity. So far as they respectively owned land, the patents simply confirmed to them *in common with their associates, the freeholders and inhabitants, their particular lots and estates.* Even if the individuals named in the second and third patents had supposed that the grants were made for their personal benefit, that could not change the legal meaning and effect of the patents, or the rights therein granted and vested and the obligations imposed.

See cases above cited. Also copies of the patents in full (Appendix C.) And the acts of Colonial Assembly and Council of 1772, 1774 and 1775, to establish and settle the line or lines of division between the City of New York and the Town of Harlem.

CHAPTER V.

THE FIRST HARLEM FARM.

Montagne's Flat and Montagne's Point.

This was alloted to and settled upon by Henry de Forest. He and his brother Isaac sailed from the Trexel October 1st, 1636, in the yacht Rensselaerwyck, and arrived at New Amsterdam, before the winter of that year set in. He had been recently married and was accompanied by his bride. He at once obtained an allotment of two hundred acres of land, from Director Wouter Van Twiller, the successor of Director Minuit. He located on the "Northeast end of the Island" on the "Flat lands" at the foot of the hills and between two kills. He immediately went into possession, and began the erection of improvements. "During the winter a farm-house was begun in the Dutch style, forty-two feet long by eighteen feet wide, with two doors, the roof was thatched, and as a protection against the Indians, the house was surrounded by a high, close fence of heavy, rounded pickets. The enclosure was ample for out-buildings, including a house for curing tobacco."

De Forest died in July of the following summer, leaving his widow, but no children surviving him. His friend Johannes Montagne had arrived from Holland the previous January, and took charge of De Forest's farm after his decease and finished the house and barn and harvested the crops.

Riker's Hist. Id. pp. 101, 139, 143.

The next year Andries Hudde, an ex-member of Van Twiller's council, married the widow of De Forest. He applied to Director Kieft, the successor of Van Twiller, in right of his wife and obtained a ground brief for the farm.

Doc. Colonial Hist. of N. Y., Vol. 14, p. 11.

The following is a copy of the deed:

"Patent for a tract of land at Harlem, New York. We, the Director and Council of New Netherland, &c., &c., herewith testify and declare, that by virtue of the Freedom and

Exemptions granted to Patroons, Masters and private persons, on the 7th day of June, 1639, we have granted, transferred, ceded and conveyed, as lawful, true and free possession, as we herewith transfer, cede, surrender and convey to and for the behoof of *Andries Hudde*, a piece of land containing one hundred morgens, situate upon the northeast of the Island, the Manhattas, *behind Curler's land*, on the condition that he and his successors shall acknowledge the aforesaid Lords Directors as their masters and patroons, and pay, after the end of ten years, commencing with the occupation or cultivation of the lands which he owns, the tenth part of the produce given to the land by God, and from this time forth for the house and lot deliver annually at Christmas to the Director, a brace of fat capons; constituting and substituting the aforesaid *Hudde* in our place and stead, real and actual possession thereof, and at the same time giving him full and irrevocable power, authority, and special charge, *tamquam actor et procurator in rem suam ac proprium*, that the said land by the said Hudde, or who thereafter may obtain his interest may be entered upon peaceably, settled, occupied, cultivated, held, used and also therewith and thereof be done, bargained and disposed of, as he would do with his own lands acquired by legal titles, without they, the grantors, in their said quality thereto having or reserving any part, action, ownership other than before recited, but for the behoof aforesaid, now and forever wholly and lastingly desisting, renouncing and withdrawing by these presents, and moreover promising this their conveyance forever firmly and inviolably and irrevocably to maintain, carry out, and fulfill, all under the rules of the law, without reservation or deceit, and in good faith. In testimony whereof we have confirmed this by our usual signature under seal.

"Done at Fort Amsterdam in New Netherland in the Manhattas, this 20th day of July 1638.

"WILLIAM KIEFT, Director."

Note on the same page. "This tract originally in the possession of Henry De Forest (who died in 1637) came by the marriage of his widow, with Andries Hudde, into the possession of the latter. Its Indian name Muscota, means a flat, and it was later known as Montagne's Flat." O'Callaghan (Hist. of New Netherland), in referring to the farm, says (Vol. 1, p. 185): "On Manhattan Island, Montagne, and other private individuals were beginning to make improvements August 1638." And on page 186, note 1. "La Montagne's farm was called Vredendael, or Valley of Peace. It belonged to Hendrick de Forest, deceased, and cost 1800 guilders or $720. This farm was one hundred morgens or two hundred acres in superfices. It is described as lying between the hills and kills *and at a point called Rechawanes situate between two kills*."

"Alb. Rec. G. G. 51, Vol. 1, 65.

"Vol. 2, 33. Vol. 3, 419."

This tract is also mentioned in Brodhead's Hist. of N. Y. under date of July 20th, 1638, Vol. 1, p. 279, in the following terms: "Near Corlears Hook on Manhattan Island, a plantation was bought by Andries Hudde, the first Commissary of Wares, and La Montagne and others began to make improvements." And in a note on same page, "Montagne's farm on Manhattan Island was called Vredendael, or Peaceful Vale. It was between Eighth Avenue and Harlem River."

Holland Doc. Vol. 8, p. 3251. See note on p. 759.

The designation near "Corlears Hook" by the historian, is misleading. This was the name of the well-known point at the junction of Cherry and Walnut Streets. The land intended to be described was Curler's Hook, or, as it was afterwards called Van Keulen's Hook, the names of the first and second owners of the point of land bounded on the South by the Harlem Creek, and on the East by the Harlem River. In regard to this land, Riker says in his history (pp. 132, 141): "Of those who early manifested an interest in this particular section (*i. e.*, Harlem) were Wouter Van Twiller, now Director-General of the colony and his friend Jacobus Van Curler, who bore the title of Jonkheer. They were both young men from the same place, Nieukerck, and Van Curler had accompanied the new Director hither in

1633. A residence of three years giving them an opportunity to spy out the land, Van Twiller had improved it by selecting for himself several choice tracts in the vicinity of New Amsterdam, among which was the island over against the Flat, Ward's Island. The Jonkheer in his rambles had fixed his covetous eyes upon these rich Flats, and with leave of the Director, had pre-empted a goodly section bordering upon the river, opposite the island referred to, and which obtained the name of Otter Spoor or Otter-track." This selection was according to this statement made in 1636; but no formal grant was then given for the land. It appears that Van Curler did not go into possession until after De Forest had begun his improvements.

Riker says: "However, Jonkheer Van Curler now set about improving his fine tract of two hundred acres, lying next to the De Forest plantation, but to describe it in familiar terms, situate North of Mill Creek at 108th Street, and extending from Harlam River to near Fifth Avenue. He erected a dwelling house and out-buildings, and procured all things necessary for a well-regulated plantation, with the no less needful boat and fixtures, for passing to and from New Amsterdam." This account of the Van Curler tract is given for the purpose of locating more definitely the property embraced in the deed to Hudde.

The outlying lands were of little value without inhabitants, and the government was not much concerned as to the amount of land taken or its precise location, provided it was actually occupied and improved by desirable settlers. This accounts for the want of precision as to the boundaries of the early farms, and the quantity of land they contained.

As there was, aside of the Indian trails, no mode of communication by land with New Amsterdam, most of the intercourse was carried on by water. It is, therefore, highly improbable that De Forest failed to avail himself of this advantage in selecting the site for his farm and future home. With the exception of the tract recently assigned to Van Curler, the whole territory was open to him. The Point Rechawanes, was the only mode of passing by land to the river, from that part of the flat lands. The kill on the northerly side of the Point provided a safe harbor for boats. The Point was bordered by the salt meadows so highly prized by the Dutch farmer. The point was an almost indispensable adjunct to the farm. The ground brief granted to Dr. John Montagne shows that this Point was in fact included in the grant to De Forest. The estate of De Forest was indebted to Montagne for advances made in the improvement and management of the farm. The Director and Council sitting as a Court ordered the property to be sold at auction in payment of the debts due by De Forest's estate. Montagne became the purchaser, and the property was conveyed to him by the following description:

"We, William Kieft, Director-General and the Council, residing in New Netherland on behalf of the High and Mighty Lords the States General of the United Netherlands of Orange and the Honorable Messieurs, the Managers of the Incorporated West India Company, do by these presents acknowledge and declare that we on this day, the date under-written, have given and granted unto Sieur Johannes La Montagne, Counsellor of New Netherland, a piece of land situate on the Island of Manhattan, known by a name in the Indian language, which in the Nether Dutch signifies *Flat Lands*, containing one hundred *morgen* in the flat, lying between the hills and kill, and a point named Rechawanes, stretching betwixt two kills, till to the East River (which above described land was occupied by Hendrick de Forest deceased, and has been purchased by said La Montagne at public auction in the Fort for seventeen hundred guilders), with express conditions and terms that he, Johannes La Montagne, or whoever by virtue hereof may accept his action shall acknowledge the Honorable Managers aforesaid as his Lords and Patroons, under the sovereignty of their High Mightiness the Lords States General, and obey their Director and Council here in all things, as good inhabitants are in duty bound to do; provided further that they subject themselves to all such burdens and imposts as are already enacted, or may hereafter be enacted by their Honors; constituting therefor the said Sieur La

Montagne, or whoever may obtain his action, in our stead in real and actual possession of the aforesaid lot and land, giving him by these presents full power, authority and special order the aforesaid parcel of land to enter upon and cultivate, inhabit and use, as he would lawfully do with other his patrimonial lands and effects, without me the grantors in the quality aforesaid, thereunto having reserved or saving any, even the slightest part, action or control whatever, but to the behoof as aforesaid, from all desisting, from now henceforth and forever. Promising moreover, this transport firm, inviolable and irrevocable to keep, respect, and fulfill, all under the penalty provided therefor by law. In witness these presents are by us signed, and confirmed by our seal in red wax hereto appended.

"Done at the Fort Amsterdam, in New Netherland, the 9th day of May, 1647.

William Kieft."

Riker's History of Harlem, p. 166. See Map, Appendix I, showing these farms and surrounding territory.

This deed was not delivered until nearly ten years after the disastrous Indian war that was instigated by the wrong headed obstinacy of Director Kieft, in February, 1643, and not brought to a close until the formal treaty of peace, made with the Indians at Fort Amsterdan in August, 1645. The Indian troubles resulted in the desolation of all the farms in Harlem. The beautiful Flats became barren wastes, and a similar fate was shared by nearly all the outlying settlements. Many of the farmers and their families were murdered, and the surviving population fled to the Fort and its vicinity for safety. "On the Island of Manhattan, from the North until the Fresh Water (*i. e.* Collect Pond, now the site of the City Prison) there is not more at this date, than five or six places inhabited; these are threatened by the Indians every night with fire, and by day by the slaughter of both people and cattle."

Holland Documents, Vol. 3, p. 134, &c.
O'Callaghan's Hist. Vol. 1, p. 294.

CHAPTER VI.

The Village of New Harlem.

The desultory warfare which followed the formal treaty of peace of 1645, discouraged the settlers from re-occupying their deserted farms. This ultimately brought about the founding of the Village of New Harlem in 1658. The establishment of the village is related by O'Callaghan and Brodhead, but Riker gives the most substantial and satisfactory account. He says (page 186): "As to the Zegendal lands and others adjacent, the Director and Council, with a just regard for all the interests involved, both of a public and private nature, resolved upon forming a village there, by laying out suitable building and forming lots to be sold to settlers at a fixed price per *morgen*, and to apply the moneys so derived for the benefit of the late proprietors, their heirs or creditors. The Van Keulen tract, besides the Kuyter lands (*i. e.*, Zegendal) was to be disposed of, with the Swits bouwery lying between them, and the cleared portion of the latter was fixed upon as the village site. As Stuyvesant owned a fourth part of the Kuyter tract, he reserved his share, probably to avoid unpleasant complications, so that only 150 *morgen* of this tract were laid out into lots. These lands being deemed ample for the wants of the proposed village for some time to come, the Vredendal, or Montagne's farm, was not as yet included; in fact, it was held that it could not from thence be conveniently cultivated, being over a kill."

"The government had another important object in view besides that of obtaining its dues or promoting the settlement of this district. This was to enhance the safety of the city of New Amsterdam, as would naturally result from the planting of a strong village with a garrison on this frontier end of the island. But in carrying out this design, neither the honest efforts of the late owners to comply with the terms of their grants by improving their lands, nor their misfortunes and losses were lost sight of. True, those lands had been granted subject to the condition that the soil should be brought under tillage. . . . Under the Dutch rule it had always been held "that a private farm or plantation ought never to be prejudicial to a village." It was under this conjunction of circumstances that called forth the following ordinance:—

"The Director-General and Council of New Netherland hereby give notice that for the promotion of agriculture, the security of this Island and the cattle pasturing thereon, as well as for the further relief and expansion of this City Amsterdam, in New Netherland, they have resolved to form a new Village or Settlement, at the end of this Island, and about the land of Jochem Peterson, deceased, and those which are adjoining to it.

"In order that the lovers of agriculture may be encouraged, the proposed new village aforesaid is favoured by the Director-General and Council with the following Privileges:

"First: Each of the inhabitants thereof shall receive by lot, in full ownership, 18 or 20 to 24 *morgen* of arable land; 6 to 8 *morgen* of Meadow (*i. e.*, salt marsh); and be exempt from tenths for fifteen years, commencing next May, on condition that he pay within the course of three years, in installments, Eight guilders for each *morgen* of tillable land for the behoof of the interested or their creditors, who are now or formerly were driven from the aforesaid lands, and have suffered great loss thereon.

"Secondly: In order to prevent similar damage from calamities or expulsions, the Director-General and Council promise the Inhabitants of the aforesaid Village to protect and maintain them with all their power, and when notified and required, to assist them with twelve to fifteen soldiers on the monthly pay of the Company, the Village providing quarters and rations. This whenever the inhabitants may petition therefor.

"Thirdly: When the aforesaid Village has 20 to 25 families, the Director-General and Council will favour it with an inferior Court of Justice; and for that purpose a double number is to be nominated out of the most discreet and proper persons, for the first time by the Inhabitants and afterwards by the Magistrates thereof, and presented annually to the Director-General and Council to elect a single number thereof.

"Fourthly: The Director-General and Council promise to employ all possible means that the inhabitants of the aforesaid Village, when it shall have the above-mentioned number of families, will be accommodated with a good, pious, orthodox minister, toward whose maintenance the Director-General and Council promise to pay half the salary, the other half to be supplied by the inhabitants in the best and easiest manner, with the advice of the Magistrates of the aforesaid Village, at the most convenient time.

"Fifthly: The Director-General and Council will assist the Inhabitants of the aforesaid Village, whenever it will best suit their convenience, to construct with the Company's negroes, a good wagon road from this place to the Village aforesaid, so that people can travel hither and thither on horseback and with a waggon.

"Sixthly: In order that the advancement of the aforesaid new Village may be the sooner and better promoted, the Director-General and Council have resolved and determined not to establish or allow to be established, any new Village or settlement, before and until the aforesaid Village be brought into existence; certainly until the aforesaid number of inhabitants is completed.

"Seventhly: For the better and greater promotion of neighborly correspondence with the English of the North, the Director-General and Council will at a more convenient time authorize a ferry and a suitable scow, near the aforesaid Village, in order to convey over cattle and horses, and will favour the Village with a cattle and horse market.

"Eightbly: Whoever are inclined to settle themselves there or to take up Bouweries by their servants, shall be bound to enter their names at once, or within a short time, at the office of the Secretary of the Director-General and Council, and begin immediately with others to place upon the land one able-bodied person, provided with proper arms, or in default thereof, to be deprived of his right.

"Thus done in the meeting of the Director and Council held in Fort Amsterdam, in New Netherland, on the 4th of March, A.D. 1658."

"The land of Jochem Peterson," mentioned in this Ordinance has reference to a tract of land granted to Jochem Peterson Kuyter. It is described as a "farm of about 400 acres at Schorrakin," or as he called it Zegendael (Vale of Blessing). It was located along the Harlem River from about 125th Street to 148th Street, and running back inward to 5th and 8th Avenues. Kuyter's house on this farm was burned by the Indians, and we have the following interesting account of the affair in a "Declaration concerning the destruction of Jochem Peterson Kuyter's house by Indians."

"This day, the 9th of March 1644, before me Cornelius Van Tievenhoven, Secretary of New Netherland appeared the under-written persons, who each for himself, at the request of Jochem Peterson Kuyter, attest, testify and declare, n place and with the promise of a solemn oath if need be, and thereunto required that their declaration is true.

"Cornelis Cornellissen, from Utrecth, aged 22 years, declares that he stood sentry on the night of the 5th of March in front of the house of said Jochem Peterson being about two hours before day, near the corn rick, about fifty paces from the barn, when he, the deponent, saw a burning arrow, the flame whereof was as blue as the flame from sulphur, coming about twenty paces from the house, between the dung hill and the cherry door, which arrow fell on the thatch of the house ; and in consequence of the violent wind, the house was immediately wrapped in flames. He immediately heard the report of a gun in the same quarter that the arrow came from. The house was burned to the ground. Also that the English soldiers during the burning would not come out of the cellar, where they were sleeping, and remained therein till the house was destroyed. Wherefore they obtained no help from the English."

This statement is corroborated by Jan Hageman, aged 22 years ; Peter Jansen, aged 24 years ; Jacob Lambersen, aged 20 years ; Dirck Gerritsen, aged 20 years.

Colonial Hist. of N. Y., Vol. 14, p. 53

Kuyter was subsequently one of the *Schepens* (Council), and at the time of his death was *Schout* (Sheriff). He afterwards built another house on his farm, and was murdered in it by the Indians in 1654.

Documentary Colonial Hist. of N. Y., Vol. 14, p. 53.

The family of John Montagne desired to establish a settlement or village on their desolated farm " Vredendael ; " and presented the following petition to the Director and Council:

"To the Noble, Great and Worshipful, the Director-General and High Council in New Netherland, Represent with due respect John de La Montagne, Junior, Jacob Kip, who married the daughter of La Montagne, Senior, and William de La Montagne, for themselves and on behalf of the absent heirs, *the true proprietors according to the letters Patent of the land lying back of New Harlem, called Vredendael, or commonly Montagne's Land*, which is situated nearly a mile from New Harlem. And, Whereas from there it can not be conveniently cultivated, lying beyond a kill, whereon in time a water-mill for the use of said village can, and as they are informed, is actually to be made ; and whereas they the petitioners, for whose greater convenience it will not only serve, in the cultivation of their land there, but will be for the better protection of the village of New Harlem, as for the benefit of the said Mill, and also afford a resting place for strangers, whether they have lost their way, or be looking for their cattle, or any others—are inclined to form there a concentration of six, eight or ten families, to remain under the jurisdiction of New Harlem, in similar manner as this has been granted by your Honors to others ; they therefore with all respect petition that they may be allowed to establish such a concentration there *either on the point of the flat land, opposite the place where the mill is to be built*, or on the heights, near the spring, or otherwise wherever your Honors may deem most proper within the jurisdiction of New Harlem, which if your Honors are pleased to permit, they promise to settle there before the next winter, six, eight or ten families.

"Praying your Honors favourable consideration of this request, we remain your Honors' servants.

"LA MONTAGNE, JUNIOR,
JACOB KIP,
WILLIAM DE LA MONTAGNE.

"July 4, 1661."

The petition was refused upon the following grounds:—
"The request is dismissed, because it is tending to the great prejudice and retarding of the Village of Harlem; and is also contrary to the privileges granted to said village some years ago." The decision was satisfactory to the inhabitants of Harlem. The village had been steadily growing, and at the close of 1661 contained over thirty adult male residents, mostly heads of families and freeholders.

The following are the names of these pioneers:

Michael Zyperus, Jan La Montagne, Jr., Daniel Tourneur, Jean Le Roy, Pierre Cresson, Jaques Cresson, Philippe Casier, David Uzille, Jaques Cousseau, Philippe Presto, Francois Le Sueur—Frenchmen.

Simon de Ruine, David Du Four, Jean Gervoe, Jan de Pre—Walloons.

Dirck Claessen, Jan Sneden, Michiel Jance Huyden, Lubbert Gerritsen, Meyndert Coorten, Aert Pietersen Buys, Segismundus Lucas—Hollanders.

Jan Pietersen Slot, Nicolaes De Heyer, Jan Lawrens Duyts, Jacob Elderts Brouwer—Danes.

Nelis Matthyssen, Morris Peterson Staeck, Jan Cogn—Swedes.

Adolph Meyer, Adom Dericksen, Hendrick Karstens—Germans.

The influx of settlers at the new village had become so large that the demand for land caused the Director and Council to issue the following Order:

"All Inhabitants of New Netherlands, especially those

of the Village of New Harlem, with all others who have or claim any lands thereabouts, are ordered and commanded, that within the space of three months from the date hereof, or at least before the first of January next, they shall have all the cultivated and uncultivated lands which they claim surveyed by the sworn Surveyor, and set off and designated by the proper marks; and on the exhibition of the return of survey thereof, apply for and obtain a regular patent as proof of property, on pain of being deprived of their right: To the end that the Director-General and Council may dispose, as they deem proper, of the remaining land which after the survey may happen to fall outside the patents, for the accommodation of others. All are hereby warned against loss and after complaints.

"This done in Fort Amsterdam in New Netherland, the fifteenth of September, 1661."

Governor Stuyvesant determined, in order to supply this demand, to disregard some of the former ground Briefs, and among others Van Keulen's Hook and Montagne's Flat. Dr. John de La Montagne was indebted to the Government, and it was arranged that he should give up that part of his farm Vredendael known as the Flat, and that his son John should retain the Point Rechawanes, and take his full allotment there, and give up his allotment No. 1, on Jochem Pieters' land, and as a special immunity should enjoy the Point free from any future demands for town taxes. He was not to build or live upon the Point until the town saw fit to allow it. The Point was rated at 16 *morgen*. His brother William was entitled to draw an allotment of 16 *morgen* of Montagne's Flat, and the debt of Dr. Montagne was liquidated.

Riker's History, pp. 200–209.

This arrangement had the effect of casting some doubt upon the title to the Montagne's Point Farm. For although it was set over to John Montagne, the younger, as the son and successor of his father, the title remained apparently in Dr. John Montagne, in the absence of an express grant from him or the Director and Council.

The forfeiture of Dr. John Montagne's property no doubt extinguished, technically, the title to both Montagne's Flat and Montagne's Point. So that John Montagne, the younger, had no paper title to the Point Farm. The titles to these two farms having been forfeited, reverted to the Government.

That was the condition of affairs at the time of the British occupation in 1664. John Montagne was in possession of the Point under claim of title. The legal title was in the Dutch Government. By virtue of the surrender to Governor Nicolls that title passed to the Duke of York; Governor Nicolls, as agent of the duke, granted the territory of Harlem to the Freeholders and Inhabitants of that town, and with that grant went the title to the Point Farm, subject to the equitable claim of John Montagne, Jr. He obtained the following deed from the Town authorities:

"We, the Magistrates, *with the vote and resolution of the Inhabitants of this Town*, have granted forever and *as hereditary*, to John de La Montagne, a piece of land, *with the meadows thereto annexed*, named Montagne's Point, formerly possessed by his late father, lying within our Town's jurisdiction, bounded on the North side by a creek called Montagne's Kill; extending from the East River unto a little fresh-water creek, running between Montagne's Flat and aforesaid Point; on the South side bounded by a creek, and a meadow and by hills, to the aforesaid little fresh-water creek, where the King's Majesty, his highway goes over, with the Meadows in the bend of Hellgate which Montagne before named has had in exchange for the Town Lots meadows; with such rights and privileges as are granted us by patent and still remain to grant, provided he submit to such laws and servitudes as with us are common, and may be imposed, without that we or our Inhabitants now or in future days, shall have any claim thereupon, but as his other patrimonial property, may enter upon or use or sell, as he may resolve and shall choose savings the lord's right. For further security, and that our deed shall have greater force and legal authority, we the Magistrates and Constable the same subscribe, this 8th day of February, Anno 1672, in New Harlem.

"D. TOURNEUR,
RESOLVERT WALDRON,
JOHANNES VERMELJE,
DAVID DES MOREST,
PETER RAELEFSEN, Constable."

Riker's Hist., Id. pp. 192, 265, 288, 211.

The effect of this deed was to remove the restrictions as to building and living upon the property, to make it subject to taxes, and entitle it to a share on the distribution of the Common Lands. (See this deed, Appendix B, 2).

In addition to the lands included in the above boundaries, the deed grants and confirms Montagne's title to "The Meadows in the Bay of Hellgate." If there should be any lingering doubt in the mind of any one, owing to the fact that the grant to Dr. John Montagne having been made by the government, the creeks would not pass by presumption, that doubt would not apply to the title derived under the deed, by the Town of Harlem, to John Montagne the younger. Whatever title the state had in the creeks passed under the Harlem Patents. The deed of the town bounded the property on the North by Montagne's Kill, and carried the title to the centre of it. It conveyed the land on both sides of the southerly creek, which formed the division between Montagne's Point and the Meadows in the Bay of Hellgate, and therefore included the whole of the bed of that creek.

See cases cited post.

The history of this title is continued post, under the head of The McGown Marshes.

CHAPTER VII.

Tidal Creeks.

PART FIRST.

Not all streams in which the tide ebbs and flows are *prima facie* navigable and public.

To raise the presumption that they are public, there must be a public use or navigation.

A private navigation may exist in tidal streams.

The theory that all tidal streams are *prima facie publici juris* is not sustained by the English Common Law authorities.

The treatise *de jure maris* is probably responsible for that theory, but it does not really teach that doctrine.

The salt marshes and the intersecting creeks are *prima facie* private property.

Common law definition of navigable rivers.

The interpretation of the deeds from Kieft, Director-General, to Dr. John Montagne and from the town of Harlem to John Montagne, the younger, involves an examination of the law applicable to tidal creeks.

The deed to Dr. John Montagne conveys the two tracts Montagne's Flat and Montagne's Point.

The land described as being between the hills and a kill, being the former tract and the land described as "the point named Rechawanes, stretching between two kills, till to the East River," being the latter tract. In construing these deeds, the first question which arises is as to the proper location of the boundary lines on the water courses. That involves an examination of the character of the streams and of the rules of law applicable to the interpretation of grants of land bordering upon small tidal streams.

The "kills" mentioned in the deeds were the outlets of small fresh water brooks or rivulets in which the tide ebbed and flowed for a few hundred yards, and they were of moderate width, depth, and navigability. They were capable of floating vessels of small tonnage at high tide and possessed a limited amount of navigable capacity. They were not arms of the sea or of the East River. That they were not arms of that river, may be inferred from the language of the grant, which describes the point as "stretching betwixt two kills till to the East River." These creeks were not so situated as, or large enough, to raise the presumption that they were public navigable rivers. If they had been without doubt, public navigable rivers, there would be no difficulty in fixing the boundary lines of the lands mentioned in the deed at the line of the ordinary high tide. If they had been wholly fresh water, not navigable streams, the boundary lines would with equal certainty be the thread of the streams.

It is the presence of the ebb and flow of the tide in small creeks and streams like those under consideration that causes the embarrassment as to the rights of the riparian owners of lands bordering on them. This is largely owing to a misapprehension of the law applicable to such streams.

From a remote period the littoral proprietors had certain proprietary rights or interests in the seashore, the sea, and some tidal waters, which rights became involved with the common law of England. Many of these property rights probably grew out of occupation, appropriation and immemorial custom.

Bracton says: "Occupancy was the source of title to the sea and the seashore and pearls and gems, and other things found there, as well as islands which spring up in the sea, and derelict goods, belong to the occupant."

Gould, *supra*, p. 6.

Blackstone says (Vol. 1, p. 62): "The municipal law of England or the rule of civil conduct prescribed to the inhabitants of this kingdom, may with sufficient propriety be divided into two kinds. The *lex non scripta*, the unwritten or common law, and the *lex scripta*, the written or statute law. The *lex non scripta*, or unwritten law, includes not only general customs, or the common law properly so called, but also the particular customs of certain parts of the kingdom, and likewise those particular laws that are by custom observed only in certain Courts and jurisdictions . . . . (p. 64.) However, I therefore style these parts of our law *leges non scriptae*, because their original constitution and authority are not set down in writings as acts of parliament are, but they receive their binding power and the force of laws by long and immemorial usuage, and by their universal reception throughout the kingdom." After the statement by the commentator that King Edward the Confessor probably extracted one uniform law or digest of laws to be observed throughout the whole kingdom from the Dome Book of King Alfred and from the Mercen and West Saxon and Dane Lage, he proceeds (p. 65) : "But through this is the most likely foundation of this collection of maxims and customs, yet the maxims and customs so collected are of higher antiquity than memory or history can reach, nothing being more difficult than to ascertain the precise beginning and the first spring of an ancient and long established custom. Whence it is that in our law the goodness of a custom depends upon its having been used time out of mind; or, in the solemnity of our legal phrase, 'time whereof the memory of man runneth not to the contrary.' This it is that gives it its weight and authority, and of this nature are the maxims and customs which compose the common law, or *lex non scripta*, of this kingdom."

As any discussion on the subject of tidal waters, without the aid of the treatise *De Jure Maris* (attributed to Lord Hale), would seem to be incomplete, that work will be first referred to. Serious doubts having arisen in recent years, as to whether the author of this work was really Lord Hale or some other person, and of its being a true exposition of the common law, its maxims should be carefully weighed and compared with acknowledged authorities, before accepting its conclusions.

See speech of Sergeant Mereweather in *Att'y-Genl.* v. *Mayor of London.*
Jerwood's reply to Sergeant Mereweather.

Hall's Sea Shores, 2d Ed. App. 68.
Gould on Waters, 108 and note 3, p. 109.
Houck on Rivers, p. 17.

Mr. Gould, in speaking of the treatise, says (p. 108): "The authorship of the work would not, perhaps, be of importance, were it not for the fact that, being associated with Lord Hale, the positions here taken have been frequently accepted as a sufficient authority without inquiry whether the positions themselves had a sound basis. The work is posthumous, and there appears to be no evidence that it was revised or intended for publication, or at what period of the author's life it was written, while Lord Hale's name has not made it in all respects incontrovertible."

Mr. Gould then states (note 3, p. 109): "In the light of modern decisions, the following rules laid down in this treatise are not law. First: That the realm of England extends beyond low water mark, and includes the adjacent seas, whether they are within the body of a county or not. Second: That any man may justify the removal of a common nuisance, either at land or by water, because every man is concerned in it. Third: That *alluvion is de jure communi* by the law of England, the king's, viz.: if by any marks or measures it can be known what is gained. Fourth: It is now established that the right of towage along the banks of rivers does not exist in the absence of usage, grant, etc., notwithstanding the intimation in this book, that this is a common-law right. The view that has been expressed in this country, that this treatise is of so high authority that there is no appeal from it (6 Cowen, 536), would appear, therefore, to be somewhat exaggerated."

Mr. Houck says (p. 18, Id.): "Deprived of Lord Hale's great name, the law as laid down in the treatise referred to, in relation to rivers, would hardly ever have been recognized in this country. It was the name of that great jurist that dazzled our judges and caused some of them to disregard the plainest principles of common reason." The treatise should be construed as a whole and in connection with other authorities. When this is done it will not appear to conflict with them.

Even Mr. Houck seems to concede this. He says (Navigable Rivers in England, p. 19):

"The doctrine here laid down seems to be in conflict with that of Bracton. Bracton says all rivers are public: The author of *De Jure Maris* says that fresh rivers, of what kind soever, belong to the owners of the soil. These two authorities on the ancient Common Law seem here to differ. Yet, when properly understood, they are entirely harmonious and consistent. The same difficulty occurs here as among French authors on the same subject. In France, navigable rivers belong to the king; rivers not navigable to the riparian owners. When this fact is borne in mind, all the French writers are reconciled with each other; but without this knowledge they seem to be in conflict.

"The truth is, that Bracton and the author of *De Jure Maris* are speaking of different subjects. Bracton is to be understood as speaking of navigable rivers, while in *De Jure Maris* rivers not navigable are considered. That Bracton is to be understood in this sense is plain from the context. He says that rivers and ports are public, and all persons are at equal liberty to land their vessels, unload them, and fasten their cables to the trees upon their banks, as to navigate the river itself. He is speaking of rivers that can be used for navigation; these are by the common law, he says, public."

The treatise *De Jure Maris* has given rise to such a contrariety of legal opinions and decisions, both in England and the United States, that it may be seriously doubted whether it was an unmixed gain to the science of law. This diversity of legal thought and authority is more apparent in the United States than in England. The difference is no doubt owing to the changed conditions and requirements of this country, and to the distance by which our legal luminaries are removed from the sources of knowledge and the traditions that are available to their brethren on the other side of the Atlantic. The paragraph, in the fourth chapter, relating to the flow and re-flow of the tide, the arms of the sea, and to public rivers, have probably been more frequently cited and discussed by courts, commentators and lawyers, than any statements of like length between the covers of any law book in the English language, and they have caused a commensurate diversity of opinions. The treatise will now be considered in connection with the interpretation of the deed by the Director Kieft to Dr. Johannes Montagne and the deed by the Freeholders and Inhabitants of Harlem to John Montagne, the younger.

Chapter IV. is entitled "Concerning the king's interest in salt water, the sea and its arms, and the soil thereof." It proceeds :—

"This much concerning fresh waters or inland rivers, which, though they empty themselves immediately into the sea, are not called arms of the sea, either in respect of the distance or smallness of them."

This description would include such streams as those under consideration for their whole length to the bank at the end of the marsh, where they emptied into the East River, which is an arm of the sea. Strictly speaking they were small rivers or rivulets for their whole length from the point where they issued from the ground until they mingled with the East River.

The next paragraph treats of the sea and the arms thereof.

"The sea is either that which lies within the body of a county or without. The arm or branch of the sea which lies within the *fauces terræ*, where a man may reasonably discern between shore and shore, is or at least may be within the body of a county, and therefore within the jurisdiction of the sheriff or coroner. The part of the sea which lies not within the body of the county is called the main sea or ocean. The narrow sea adjoining the coast of England is part of the waste and *demesne* and dominions of the King of England, whether it lie within the body of a county or not."

"For the second, that is called an arm of the sea where the sea flows and re-flows, and so far only as the sea flows and re-flows; so that the river Thames above Kingston, and the river Severn above Tewkesbury, though they are public rivers, yet are not arms of the sea. But it seems that although the water be fresh at high water, yet the denomination of an arm of the sea continues if it flow and re-flow as in the Thames above the bridge."

If, under this test (wherever the tide flows and re-flows), it is claimed that the water is public, then every small creek in which a fishing skiff or gunning canoe can be made to float at high water, as Chief Justice Shaw expresses it in *Rowe* v. *Granite Bridge Corp.*, (21 Pick. 344), is *prima facie* a navigable public stream.

The mere statement of such a proposition is enough to give an impression of its absurdity.

A further examination of the treatise will show that such small streams are not claimed to be part of the public domain.

In Chapter III, entitled "Concerning *Public Streams*," this statement is made: "There be some streams or rivers that are private, not only in propriety or ownership, but also in use, as little streams and rivers that are not a common passage for the king's people. Again there be other rivers, as well fresh as salt, that are of common or public use for carriage of boats and lighters. And these, whether they are fresh or salt, whether the tide flow and re-flow or not, are *prima facie publici juris* common highways for man or goods, or both, from one inland town to another."

It is evident that the mere presence of the tide-water does not raise the presumption that a stream or river is public. "Little streams that are not a *common passage* for the King's people" are declared to be private "*not only in ownership but in use*." Only those rivers that are "*of common or public use*" are declared to be *prima facie publici juris*. And this whether they are fresh or salt, or whether the tide flow and re-flow in them or not. Nor does the fact that the small streams are used for the occasional **passage** of vessels, of itself raise the presumption that **they are** public; but they must be "*of common or public use.*"

The following extracts from the *De Jure Maris* and *De Jure Portibus* illustrate this, namely: "But a subject hath not, or indeed can not have that proprietory in the sea, through a whole tract of it as the king hath; because without a regular power (*i. e.*, a naval force) he cannot possibly possess it. But though a subject can not acquire an interest of the narrow seas, yet he may by usage and prescription acquire an interest in so much of the sea as he may reasonably possess, viz.: of a district *maris*, a place in the sea between such points, or a particular part contiguous to the shore, or of a port or creek or arm of the sea. These may be possessed by a subject, and prescribed in point of interest both in the water, and the soil itself covered with the water, within such a precinct; for these are manoriable (*i. e.*, appertaining to a manor) and may be entirely possessed by a subject.

De Jure Maris, Chap. 6. (Gould, *supra*, p. 51).

The kind of creek referred to is beyond reasonable doubt a creek of a port or a creek connected with a port. This will be made evident upon comparing the language with the *De Portibus Maris*, relating to creeks and ports, namely: "A port is a haven and somewhat more. 1st. It is a place for arriving and unloading of ships or vessels. 2d. It hath a superinduction of a civil signature upon it, somewhat of franchise, and privilege, as shall be shown. 3d. It hath a ville or city or borough, that is the *caput portus*, for the receipt of mariners and merchants and securing and vending of their goods and victualling their ships, ... A port of the sea includes more than the bare place where the ships unlade, and sometimes extends many miles; as the port of London anciently extended to Greenwhich in the time of King Edward the first. . . . A Creek is of two kinds, viz.: creeks of the sea and creeks of ports. The former sort are such inlets of the sea whether within or without the precinct or extent of a port, which are narrow little passages and have shore of either side of them. The latter, viz.: creeks of ports, are by a kind of civil denomination such. They are such, that though *pos-*

sibly, *for their* extent and situation they might be ports, yet they are either members of, or dependent upon other ports. And it began thus: The king could not conveniently have a customer and comptroller in every port and haven; these custom officers were fixed at some convenient port, and the smaller adjacent ports became by that means creeks or appendants of that where these custom officers were placed."

De Portibus, C. 2, Hargrave's Law Tracts, 46, 48; Gould Id. pp. 5, 10, 11.

"Though of common right, the king is *prima facie*, the owner and lord of every *public* sea port, yet the subject may by charter or prescription be lord or owner of it. . . . . The ownership of propriety is where the king or common person by charter or prescription is the owner of the *soil of a creek or haven where ships may safely arrive and come to the shore*. This interest of proprietory may, as hath been shown, belong to a subject. But he hath not thereby the franchise of a port; neither can he so use or employ it unless he hath had that liberty time out of mind or by the king's charter. Though A may have the proprietory of a creek or harbor or navigable river, yet the king may grant there the liberty of a port to B, and so the interest of propriety and the interest of franchise several and divided. And in this no injury is at all done to A, for he hath what he had before, viz.: the interest of the *soil* and consequently the improvement of the shore and the liberty of fishing, and as the creek was free for any to pass in it against all but the king; for it was *publici juris* as to that matter before, so now the king takes off that restraint, and by his license and charter makes it free for all to come and unlade."

Hale's *De Portibus Maris*, C. 6.
Hargrave's Law Tracts, 73.
Gould's Watercourses, note, p. 11.

The creeks mentioned in the first classification would apparently include all creeks that are not creeks of a port.

A creek of a port is one, which owing to its shape, size, and channel and connection with other places and waters may possibly possess the requisite features for a port. Although it has not been made a port, it is nevertheless connected with, and forms part of the system of an adjacent port, and in that way is connected with a city, ville or borough. By way of illustration, the kill between Staten Island and New Jersey possesses the requisite conditions for a port, yet that stream may be said to be a creek of the port of New York. But suppose there should be a tidal creek running through the extinct New Jersey marshes, to a point on New York Bay, or on the Hudson opposite to New York, no one would think of that stream as a creek of a port.

The creek of a port being directly connected with commerce and the custom officers, would be *prima facie* a public stream. It does not necessarily follow, that a creek which "*possibly* for its extent and situation" is capable of becoming a port or member of, or dependent upon another port, but which is not so in fact, is therefore *prima facie* public. These characteristics may not be sufficient to raise that presumption. If in addition it has a broad and deep channel, calculated for the purposes of commerce, or has been used by the public time out of mind, that would probably raise the presumption that it was a public navigable channel.

Rex v. *Montague*, 4 B. & C. 598.

A creek in private ownership and possession, which has the requisite qualifications for a port, is subject to the *publici juris*, and the king may take off the restraint as to public use and establish a port upon it, and grant the franchise of a port to a stranger. The owner of the creek will still own the soil, the liberty of fishing, the improvement of the shore and his other rights; but subject to the public use under the port franchise. If a port was actually established on a creek of that kind although in private ownership, that fact would raise the presumption that the creek was subject to the public use. If a grant of land were made by the Government bordering on a creek which is a public port, it would be limited to the line of high water. If the grant were made by a private person, or civil or other corporation, being the owner of the bed of the creek, it would include the stream, unless it was reserved in express terms, or by clear intention, but the stream would be subject to the public use.

If there were no port established on such a creek, in the absence of proof that it was a public navigable channel, the creek would be *prima facie* private, and a grant of land bordering by its boundaries upon it would go by presumption of law to the thread of the stream.

See cases cited and discussed, post.

The term "creeks of the sea" would include the salt water creeks, ever present in salt marshes.

This brings up for consideration and examination the status of lands of that kind. In Ch. 6 of *De Jure Maris* they are thus classified:

"I. The shore of the sea."

There seem to be three sorts of shores, or *littora marina* according to the various tides, viz:

"1st. The high spring tides, which are the fluxes of the sea at those tides that happen at the two equinoxials, and certainly do *not de jure communi* belong to the crown. For such spring tides many times overflow *ancient meadows and salt marshes, which yet unquestionably belong to the subject, and this is admitted of all hands.*

"2d. The spring tides which happen twice every month, at full and change of the moon, and the shore in question is by some opinion not denominated by these tides, but the lands overflowed by these fluxes ordinarily belong to the subject *prima facie*, unless the king hath a prescription to the contrary. The reason seems to be because for the most part the lands covered by these fluxes are dry and manoriable, for at other tides the sea doth not cover them, and therefore touching these shores some hold that common right speaks for the subject, unless there be an usage to entitle the Crown; for this is not properly *littus maris*."

Mr. Hall in his work on Seashores, says (p. 7): "In all the marshy districts and fens along the *coasts of the sea*, creeks and tide rivers, the lands which are subject to the spring tides are of considerable extent and value, and by no means so barren and unprofitable, as the ordinary seashore or strand. The marshes are indeed in many places manoriable, as Lord Hale expressed it, *and the right to embank* and enclose them against the spring tides, *and reduce them to a completely cultivatable state*, is of no small importance to the Lords of the manor and the owners of the adjacent *terra firma*."

The salt marshes being invariably subdivided by tidal creeks of greater or less size and extent, this ownership of the marshes by the subject, with the right to enclose, embank, and cultivate them, includes the right to close up the creeks to keep out the sea water. This shows very clearly that the title to these creeks and to the soil under them is in the owners of the marshes, without any restraint. Of course if in any of the larger creeks a public right has intervened by reason of an immemorial custom, or public use, owing to which they have become subject to a public servitude, such creeks probably could not be closed. The fact of the private ownership, and absolute control over these creeks of the marshes by the subject, is a very important one. It has a direct bearing upon the question, as to the force and effect to be given to the fact, that the tide ebbs and flows in any particular stream. If the fact that it flows in the creeks of the marshes, does not raise the presumption that they are *publici juris*, because of the well-known fact, that time out of mind, these marshes and creeks have been in the private ownership of the subject, then that test is not one of universal application. The ebb and flow of the tide is not the vital test under the common law, to determine whether a river is a public navigable stream or not.

This is one of the reasons tending to show that immemorial use by the public, is the really reliable test to show that a river is public and navigable. The test is of course subject to the well known rule of law, that where a matter is of such a general and public notoriety as to be generally and publicly known, the court will take judicial notice of the fact, as that the Thames is navigable up to London Bridge.

Gould, *supra*, p. 201.

Blackstone makes only this brief statement in regard to the king's right in ports and the shore and navigable rivers, viz.: "Sir Edward Coke lays it down that no subject can build a castle, or house of strength embattled, or other fortress defensible, without the license of the king; for the danger which might ensue if every man at his pleasure might do it. It is partly upon the same and partly upon a fiscal foundation, to secure his maritime revenue, that the king has the prerogative of appointing ports and havens, or such places only, for persons and merchandise to pass into and out of the realm, as he in his wisdom sees proper. By the feudal law *all navigable* rivers and havens were computed among the regalia, and were subject to the sovereign of the state. And in England it hath always been holden, that the king is lord of the whole shore, and particularly is he the guardian of the ports and havens, which are inlets and gates of the realm; and, therefore, so early as the reign of King John, we find ships seized by the king's officers for putting in at a place that was not a *legal* port. These *legal* ports were undoubtedly at first assigned by the crown; since to each of them a court of portmote is incident, the jurisdiction of which must flow from the royal authority; the great ports of the sea, are also referred to, as well known and established by statute 4, Hen. IV., c. 20, which prohibits the landing elsewhere, under the pain of confiscation, and the statute 1, Eliz., c. 11, recites that the franchise of landing and discharging had been frequently granted by the crown."

Blackstone, Com. B. i, 263.

Judged by the context, the learned commentator, by the term *navigable rivers*, refers to rivers that are directly connected with commerce as understood by the law of nations. The rivers are directly associated with havens and *legal* ports which he terms inlets and gates of the realm; and they again are associated with the collection of the revenue or customs; and the king's lordship of the whole shore is spoken of in the same connections, and this again would seem to imply or include those shores only which are connected with actual navigation.

It is a significant fact, that no reference whatever is made to the flow and re-flow of the tide. If at the time Blackstone wrote, the ebb and flow of the tide was the important sign by which to determine whether a river was a public navigable river or not, it certainly is a most remarkable circumstance, that in such a work, no reference should have been made to a criterion of such far-reaching importance.

These extracts from English authorities will serve to show that private property in the beds of important tidal waters has existed to a large extent, and from very remote periods of time. In a country like England, with a system of laws so wise, it is not at all probable that side by side with the existence of such property rights would also have existed a law which said: "Wherever the tide ebbs and flows, *prima facie*, no such property rights exist, because the title in *all* tidal waters is in the king." This would put upon the owners of these small creeks, the burden of proving title, and put such property under a perpetual ban. This interpretation of these sections of the treatise, is in harmony with the more recent English authorities.

Lord Hale died in 1676. Assuming *De Jure Maris* to be his work, it slumbered in the archives of the British Museum until it was brought to light by Mr. Hargrave in 1787.

In the interim between the death of Lord Hale and the publication of the treatise, the exposition of the law in England did not stand still. Great jurists and eminent exponents of the law lived and died. Among these learned men was Lord Mansfield.

It may be safely assumed that no intelligent lawyer is prepared to maintain that he did not know what the law was without the aid of this treatise. In 1774, Lord Mansfied made a decision in the celebrated case of the *Mayor of Lynn* v. *Turner* (1 Cowper, p. 86), in which he says: "*Ex facto oritur jus.* How does it appear that this is a navigable river? *The flowing and re-flowing of the tide does not make it so, for there are many places into which the tide flows that are not navigable rivers;* and the place in question may be a creek in their own private estate."

Mr. Woolwych in referring to this case says, that the claim made by the corporation of Lynn, that the creek in question was public because the tide ebbed and flowed in it, was treated by the court as a fallacy.

Woolwych on Waters, p. 312, *supra.*

In *Rex* v. *Montague* (4 Barnwall & Creswall's R.). Bailey, J., says, p. 601: "It was for the defendant to make out that there once was a *public navigation. Now it does not necessarily follow, because the tide flows and re-flows in any particular place, that there is therefore a public navigation, although of sufficient size."* .... "The strength of this *prima facie* evidence, arising from the flux and re-flux of the tide must depend upon the situation and nature of the channel. *If it is a broad and deep channel, calculated for the purposes of commerce,* it would be natural to conclude that it has been a *public* navigation; but if it is a petty stream, navigable only at certain periods of the tide, and then only for a short time, and by very small boats, it is difficult to suppose that it ever has been a *public navigable channel."* The opinions of Holroyd, J., and Littledale, J., were to the same effect.

From these authorities it appears that the mere ebb and flow of the tide in a small stream is not sufficient to raise the presumption that it is public, but there must also be a public navigation, or at least a capacity for navigation, for commerce. Although a private navigation may exist in such a stream, yet the terms public navigation and public navigable channel are the equivalents of the expression in the treatise "of rivers that are of a common or public use." What is meant by a public navigation is, an open and notorious use by the public, for a sufficient time to establish a public right.

In *Vooght* v. *Winch* (2 Barnwall & Alderson's R., p. 662), on the trial it was held that "In a public navigable river, twenty years possession of the water at a given level, etc., is not conclusive as to the right, even although it had been a public navigable river."

Abbott, Chief Justice, says: "The learned judge left it to the jury, on the evidence to consider whether the stream called *Channel Sea River* was navigable, and in what way, whether as a *public navigable river, or for the convenience of the adjoining occupiers;* and he further added, that whether navigable or not, he thought each party was bound to use the water in the state in which it was found to be for the space of twenty years invariably, and that a certain benefit so long enjoyed could not afterwards be disturbed. In that decision it appears to me the learned judge was mistaken, for if it be admitted that this is a public navigable river, and that all his majesty's subjects had a right to navigate it, an obstruction to such navigation for a period of twenty years would not have the effect of preventing his majesty's subjects from using it as such." Bailey, J., said: "I am of the same opinion. I think we are not warranted in saying that there was not enough at least to go to the jury to say whether this was not a navigable river; and if it was a navigable river, then an obstruction for twenty years is not enough to bar a public right." Holyrood, J., said: "If the place in question was ever a public navigable river, I apprehend that in ceasing to use it as such for twenty years, and being during that time in a condition which is inconsistent with its being used as a *public navigable river* would not extinguish the public rights, if they ever existed previously to that time." Holyrood, J., concurred in the subsequent decision in *Rex* v. *Montague, supra.*, in which it was held that the public right in a channel might be terminated in other ways than by an act of Parliament.

The mere presence of a sloop or lighter or of small vessels in a small stream in which the tide flows, does not raise the presumption that it is a public navigable stream. In the *Mayor, &c., of Colchester* v. *Brooke* (7 Queen's Bench 372, decided in 1845), Lord Denman, C. J., says: "It is more reasonable to hold that the term *navigable* is a relative and comprehensive term, containing within it all such rights upon the waterway as, with relation to the circumstances of each river, are necessary for the full and convenient passage of boats and vessels along the channel." Lord Denman also said, in *Williams* v. *Wilcox* (8 Ad. and El. 314, 333, 1838): "It is clear that the channels of *public navigable rivers were always highways;* up to the point reached by the flow of the tide the soil was presumably in the Crown; and above that point, whether the soil at common law was in the Crown, or the owners of the adjacent lands (a point perhaps not free from doubt), there was at least a jurisdiction in the Crown, according to Sir Matthew Hale, to reform and punish nuisances, in all rivers, whether fresh or salt that *are a common passage*, not only for ships and greater vessls, but also for smaller."

Gould, *supra.*, p. 112.

In *Rex* v. *The Inhabitants of Landulph*, (1 Moody and Robinson's R. p. 393, 1834), was an indictment for non-repair of a road. The road in question led over a small inlet or estuary of Tamer River, not far from its mouth. It was not passable at high water, and was usually a soft sludge at ebb. The defense was that the road was not a public highway at all, and if any, was one in its nature not capable of repair. *It was also contended that this road was not* in the parish of Landulph. Patterson, J., held in reference to the question of boundary, "that where two parishes are separated by a river, and there is no positive evidence of the boundary line between them, it is to be presumed that they coincide with the middle of the channel." It should be here noted, that this case was subsequently criticised in an unfriendly spirit, in the case of *Bridgewater* v. *Town of Bootle*, which will be discussed presently.

In *McCannon and others* v. *Sinclair and others* (Ellis & Ellis R. p. 54, 1853), it was held, that where a parish comes down as far as the bank of a river, there is *prima facie* presumption that the parish extends as far as the middle of the river. A pier leading from the river bank in such a parish, into the river beyond the low water mark, and consisting of a fixed platform supported on piles, commencing within two or three inches from the bank, and a floating barge moored close to, but not attached to the platform, is to be held, in the absence of evidence to rebut the presumption, as being within the parish; and such a pier is ratable at the poor rate.

Lord Campbell, Ch. J., delivered the opinion. He said: "The point has very properly been argued; but we are clearly of opinion that the plaintiffs are entitled to judgment."

Mr. Gould, in discussing the case of the Royal Fishery of the Banne, decided in Ireland in 1611, says (p. 107, Id.): "The real question presented for decision was, whether a royal grant of certain lands adjacent to the river Banne conveyed a salmon fishery at a point in the river where it was *navigable*. If the word navigable as here used means *tidal*, the question of title to a fresh-water river was not in issue; and the first part of the last resolution, in which the king is held to be the owner of tidal rivers, and the resolution that nothing passed by implication in a royal grant, embrace the only points that were directly decided." And note 1, same page: "The word *navigable* in this case is, perhaps, of somewhat doubtful meaning, it being said that every navigable river, so high as the sea ebbs and flows in it," is a royal river; that every other river not navigable, and every "inland river not navigable, are private." The rivers here referred to in the second classification, beyond reasonable doubt, mean tidal rivers.

Gould, *supra.*, p. 107.

The House of Lords, in *Bristow* v. *Cormican* (3 App. Cas. 641), controverts the doctrine of the Crown's title as universal occupant of vacant land. Lord Blackburn said: "It is, however, necessary to decide whether the Crown has of common right a *prima facie* title to the soil of a lake. I think it has not. I know of no authority for saying it has, and I see no reason why it should have it. Mr. Justice Lawson in his able opinion hints at one. "What ground," he says, "is there for suggesting that the title was not in the Crown? It is not shown, or even suggested, to be in any other, and it could not be in the public." This would be a strong remark if there was any authority for saying that, by the prerogative, the Crown was entitled to all lands to which no one else can show a title. But this is so far from being the case, that in the only instance in which no one could show a title—I mean that of an estate granted to one for the life of another, where the grantee died leaving the *cestui que vie*—the law cast the freehold on the first occupant of the land. (See Co. Litt. 40.) It was never thought that the Crown was entitled in such a case. Those who committed trespasses after the death of a tenant for life, and before any one occupied, did so with impunity, because there was no one entitled to complain of their acts, and it may be that those who fish in Lough Neagh may do so not of right, yet with impunity, so long as the true owner of the soil either fails to prove his right, or does not choose to interfere. But that does not give any rights to the Crown. The Crown might have had title in many ways, by forfeiture or escheat, or otherwise, but generally speaking, in order to make such a title in the Crown perfect, there must be office found."

See Gould Id. p. 39.

In England none of the rivers in their natural conditions were navigable in the full sense of that term, above the ebb and flow of the tide. Had there been large fresh water rivers in that country capable of navigation, as on the continent of Europe and in America, the common law, without doubt, would have been adapted to the actual condition of the country. The rivers would have become "of common or public use for carriage of boats and lighters" to the whole extent of their navigability. The *De Jure Maris* treats of ancient customs and facts actually existing and which had existed for ages and had been before the courts for adjudication. If England had possessed large freshwater rivers of this character, the statement could still have been "again there are other rivers, as well fresh as salt, that are of common or public use for carriage of boats and lighters. And these, whether they are fresh or salt, whether the tide flow or re-flow or not are *prima facie publici juris*, common highway for man, or for goods, or both." The ebb and flow of the tide, however, would not have been used as the test to show to what extent the rivers were navigable.

The title of the king to the arms of the sea, and the bed of the *navigable* rivers, so far as the tide flows and re-flows, was not founded upon decrees or statutes, but upon the *lex non scripta*. His title did not extend to all the waters within the reach of the tide, but to those only which had become "of public use."

Whether the king's title does or does not extend to all tidal waters, is a question of law. If it is claimed that his title arises out of his prerogatives, or the feudal law, or upon general reception and usage, the authorities for such opinions must be produced, in order to raise the presumption that the water in controversy is public. In other words, it is strictly a common law question. It is one of those "doctrines that are not set down in any written statute or ordinance, but depend merely upon immemorial usage, that is, upon common law, for their support."

Blackstone, Com., Vol. 1, p. 68.

Blackstone tells us, 63 Id., how the law is ascertained: "But, with us at present the monuments and evidences of our legal customs are contained in the records of the several Courts of Justice, in books of reports and judicial decisions, and in the treatises of learned sages of the profession, preserved and handed down to us from the highest antiquity. However, I therefore style these parts of our law *leges non scriptae*, because their original institution and authority are not set down in writing, as the acts of parliament are, but they receive their binding power and force of laws by long immemorial usage, and their universal reception throughout the kingdom."

This test of a navigable river, arising from its use for navigation, has been in existence time out of mind. "A public navigable river," says Woolrych, "frequently owes its title to be considered as such from time immemorial, by reason of its having been an ancient stream, but very many acts of Parliament have been passed to constitute those navigable rivers which were not so before."

He says: "Rivers are either public, as where there is a common right of navigation exercised, and then the soil is in the king, or in the lord of the manor; or private, where the soil is the property of an individual who owns the land on both sides, or of each proprietor, *ad medium filum aquae*, where the same person is not the owner of the shore on either bank."

And he shows that few of the English rivers except the Thames and Severn were naturally navigable, but were made so by acts of Parliament. "Waters," he goes on to say, "flowing inland where the public have been used to exercise a free right of passage from time whereof the memory of man is not to the contrary, or by virtue of legislative enactment, are *public navigable rivers*." This he further says, "is the most *unfailing* test to apply, *in order* to ascertain a common right; others have been attempted and frequently without success."

Woolrych on Waters, pp. 31 to 33.
Houck on Rivers, p. 11, *supra*.

The common law may be said to be the outgrowth of facts. Lord Mansfield said, in the case of *Mayor of Lynn* v. *Turner*, (1 Cowper, 86 *supra*): "The law arises from the fact." And to say that every stream and river, in which the tide ebbs and flows is a public navigable river *in the law*, when very many such rivers are *not navigable in fact*, is equivalent to saying the law arises out of a theory.

The common law doctrine of the rights of littoral and riparian proprietors may be stated in the following terms: In all arms of the sea and all public navigable rivers, which are "a common passage not only for ships and great vessels but also for smaller," in which the tide ebbs and flows, the titles of the owners of the upland extends *prima facie* to the line of ordinary high tide, and in all other rivers and streams which are not so navigable, or a common passage for the king's people, whether the same are fresh or salt, or whether the tide flows in them or not, the title of such proprietors, extends *prima facie*, to the *filum aquae*, or thread of the stream.

Or the law as to what *prima facie* constitutes a navigable river or stream, may be stated in this way. No stream or river is a public navigable river in which the tide does not ebb and flow. But not that all streams and rivers in which the tide ebbs and flows are necessarily public navigable rivers. A public navigable river is one in which the tide ebbs and flows, which has a broad and deep channel, and is a common passage for the king's people, and is of common use for carriage of boats and lighters, and is a common highway for man or for goods, or for both.

Mr. Tyler in his work on the Law of Boundaries (p. 47), states the law as above defined in this manner: "It may be added, that rivers where the tide ebbs and flows, probably do not belong to the public, only in those parts which are *navigable*. So that the owners of lands adjoining a river below the ebb and flow of the tide, *if navigable*, are bound *prima facie* by the line of the high water mark; but if not *in fact navigable*, these may be presumed to own to the center of the stream." It clearly appears from these authorities, that by the rules of construction of grants of land bordering upon private streams, made by the sovereign to a subject, the title extends to the thread of the stream, unless the grant in express terms, or by implication, limits the title of the grantee to the high water line, or bank.

If a small stream like those now under consideration has from use or dedication become open to the public, the Court will not take judicial notice of the fact. "If the character of the stream is not defined in any public statute, or in a private statute introduced in evidence, and it is not of such a notoriety as to be generally understood, it can not be known judicially that it is navigable."

Gould Id., p. 201.

People v. *Allen*, 42 N. Y. pp. 378-81.
The New York and Brooklyn Saw Mill and Lumber Co. v. *The City of Brooklyn*, 71 N. Y. 580.

CHAPTER VIII.

Tidal Creeks.

PART SECOND.

According to American law to render a stream public, there must be an actual or potential use of water for some useful purpose connected with trade or agriculture.
The Constitution of the State of New York, 1777.
The American authorities as to tidal waters conflicting and discordant.
English and American authorities examined and compared.
By the common law there are three kinds of rivers.
The interpretation of grants bordering on small tidal streams.
No Court of final resort has actually decided, that as a matter of law, all streams in which the tide ebbs and flows are *prima facie* public and navigable.
The rivulets of Manhattan Island.
The Harlem salt water creeks not public streams.

It now remains to consider the question as presented by the rules of law in the United States, and particularly in the State of New York.

In this country the law seems to be, that actual or potential use of water, for purposes of navigation for some useful purpose, is the test of navigability. The ebb and flow of the tide is (as respects ownership of soil) immaterial except to raise the presumption of navigability, when it is shown by the dimensions and accessibility of the water to be practicable. Tide water flowing through a narrow crevice among rocks into a large or deep pool, would not be navigable; neither is tide water flowing into a shallow swamp. To hold otherwise would be a contradiction in terms as in fact.

The law, as by the constitution of the State of New York, of 1777 established, has not been changed by any subsequent constitution or statutes, so far as it relates to tidal waters. Opinions of Senator Verplanck, in *The Canal Commissioners* v. *Kempshal*, (26 Wend., 404,) and of Judge Gray, in *Roberts* v. *Baumgarten*, (110 N. Y., p. 380.) The constitution was adopted ten years before the treatise *De Jure Maris* was published. The decision of Lord Mansfield in the *Mayor of Lynn* v. *Turner, supra*, was delivered in 1774. It was the most recent statement of the law affecting small tidal streams and was of authority in the colony when the constitution was adopted. It has been followed in subsequent leading cases in England, as above cited. These decisions are the authoritative interpreters of the common law, and are in harmony with the *De Jure Maris*.

The deed by the Kieft, Director-General, &c., to John Montague, the elder, must be construed according to the common law, as it was when the deed was given, or at least in 1775, according to the Constitution of 1777.

In *Canal Commissioners* v. *The People*, (5 Wendell,) Senator Allen, in delivering his opinion says (p. 452): "Now although the common law as it existed in 1774 (*i. e.*, 1775), may be altered or repealed by the legislature to take effect from and after such alteration or repeal, *it cannot be so altered as to affect grants existing prior to* 1774 (*i. e.*, 1775). *Ancient grants must be expounded according to what the law was at the time of making them.* Comy's Digest, 419."

The important case of *Rogers* v. *Jones*, (1st Wendell, 238, decided in 1828), has a direct bearing on the subject of the interpretation of grants by the government.

On the 29th of September, 1677, a patent was granted by Sir Edmond Andros, then Governor of New York, under the Duke of York to Henry Townsend, senior, and six other persons as patentees, for and on behalf of themselves and their associates, the freeholders and inhabitants of Oyster Bay. The lands were bounded as follows: Bounded on the North by the Sound, on the East by the Huntington limits, on the South partly by the sea and partly by Hempstead limits, and on the West by the bounds of Hempstead aforesaid, including all the necks of land within the aforesaid bounds and limits, together with all the woodland, plains, meadows, pastures, quarries, marshes, waters, lakes, rivers, fishing, hawking, hunting and fowling, and all other profits and emoluments to the tract belonging, and all privileges and immunities belonging to a town.

Woodworth, J., delivered the opinion, and Savage, C. J., and Southerland, Asst. J., concurring, he said: "It can not be doubted that when a patent or grant conveys a tract of land by metes and bounds, the land under water as well as other land will pass, if the land under water lies within the boundaries of the grant. A contrary doctrine would exclude the lands under the water of lakes and streams not navigable. Scarcely a patent ever issued by this state, that does not include one or the other; and as far as I know, no question has ever been raised on this ground. . . . . I deem it unnecessary to cite other authorities. Many might be adduced, but enough has been shown to satisfy my mind, that the patent of Sir Edmond Andros, emanating immediately from Charles the Second, did convey to the inhabitants of Oyster Bay, all the lands under water within the bounds of that grant."

In case of *Commonwealth* v. *Charlestown*, (1 Pick., Mass., Rep. 179), shows that a tidal creek is not *prima facie* a public navigable water. The defendants proved that the channel over which a bridge was built, was seventy-four feet wide at the bridge, and nine and a half feet deep at high water; that the bridge was one hundred and ninety-six feet long; and that for more than fifty years vessels of from fifteen to thirty tons and upwards used to go above the bridge carrying West India goods to a range way on which they were carted across the meadows. There was a constant stream of fresh water entering the bed of the river, on which there is a mill above tide water. At a smaller bridge there was seven and a half feet of water in spring tides, and a channel more than a pole wide, vessels of fourteen or fifteen tons passing, while there was water enough for those of forty or fifty tons.

This case turned upon the proof that the stream had been used by the public for commercial purposes for more than fifty years. The ebb and flow of the tide did not determine the controversy.

Parker, Ch. J., delivered the opinion. He said: "The question then in the case before us, is whether the streams over which the bridges are placed are *public highways*;

if they are, the order of the Court of Sessions laying a road over them is void. If it appears from the evidence that the streams in question are navigable to any useful purpose, as that in our opinion would make them public property, the verdict ought to be set aside."

What the learned Chief Justice said in regard to common law, was not really in the case, and while it is entitled to respectful consideration, it is not binding, as matter of authority. If the common law is as the Chief Justice stated it, there was no necessity for the defendant to prove public navigation.

All the proof that was required was that the tide ebbed and flowed in the creek, and in the absence of proof of title, by grant or by prescription on the part of the plaintiff, the decision would necessarily have been that the title was *prima facie* in the state.

Four years after this, that is 1826, the celebrated case of *Ex parte Jennings* (6 Cowen, p. 528), was decided in New York. The language of the court in regard to the common law rule relating to the flow and re-flow of the tide is so similar to that of Chief Justice Parker, as to raise the impression that it was derived from his decision. It may be that both of these opinions were drawn from a common source, but neither of them appear to be in accordance with the English authorities.

The language of these, as well as that of some of the other decisions in the United States, which include all tidal waters as public, seems to show a want of harmony with the English jurisprudence on the subject.

The opinion that the king's title extends to *all* tidal waters, even the smallest creek as well the largest river, appears to be based entirely upon the above mentioned passage in the treatise *De Jure Maris*. There seems to be no authority for such a doctrine anterior to the publication of that work. It is believed that every opinion holding that to be the law, whether expressed by court or counsel, if it could be traced to its source, will be found to take its rise in the paragraph relating to the flow and re-flow of the tide in that treatise. Now it is probable that the author of that work did not mean to be so understood. But if he did, it is very strange that we do not find prior to its appearance, this doctrine stated in any such marked and pronounced language as is shown in many of the American decisions, since the *De Jure Maris* appeared.

Assuming that this hypothesis is correct, there are but two tenable theories on which to account for it, namely: First, The treatise does not teach that to be the law; or, Second; if it were the law when the treatise was written, it was not afterwards regarded or followed.

Referring to this variance from the English law, Mr. Houck says (p. 11, *supra*.):

"It is commonly received opinion in this country, that in England the only test of navigability of a river is the ebb and flow of the tide. This general idea here, on this point is, however, erroneous. It is true that there the usual means of designating a navigable river is the ebb and flow of the tide; and it is this common method of designation which has led to the idea here, that the ebb and flow of the tide is the only test of navigability at common law; but this opinion is, as already remarked, an error, because there, while it is the commonly used and most prominent, *it is not the only test* being the most natural and the most readily perceived test in that country, it was easy to take for granted without question or reflection, that it was the only test. It is, however, not reasonable to suppose that such would be the case, in a system of laws so eminently flexible as that of England, and so easily adapting itself to the necessity of circumstances controlling the application of a principle, when navigability did not depend on the ebb and flow of the tide, and the natural test stated was *by daily observation of actual navigation*, shown to be erroneous. Our general adoption of this idea here, does not make the test itself correct; nor does its general use there make it such, even there. *Wherever the public, whether in England or America, have actually used a river as navigable*, it is such, whether the tide ebbs or flows, or does not ebb or flow, at the navigable places in its course so used." He futher says (p. 15, Id.): "In some American Courts, the common law seems to have been misunderstood, and the ebb and flow of the tide is considered the only test of navigability, and misled by this idea some singular decisions have been made."

It is probable that Mr. Houck was quite right in this opinion; and that it was owing to certain passages in the treatise *De Jure Maris* that many eminent judges in this country were led to believe that the term *navigable rivers*, meant *all* waters in which the tide ebbs and flows and excluded all other waters. The unreasonbleness of this proposition as well as its unsuitableness to the conditions existing in this country, led some of the judges to modify or wholly repudiate the supposed common law, as inapplicable to this country. This is shown in the following opinions. Judge Bronson said in *Child* v. *Starr*, (20 Wendell, 149): "Navigable rivers belong to the public; other streams may be owned by individuals. . . . . In England, a rule of evidence has been adopted, which although it recognizes the doctrine, does not always give it complete practical effect. By the common law, the flow and re-flow of the tide is the criterion for determining what rivers are public.

"This rule is open to the double objection, that it includes some streams which are not in fact navigable, and which consequently might well be subject to individual ownership; and it excludes other streams, which are in fact navigable, and which in every well regulated State should belong to the public.

"Although the ebb and flow of the tide furnishes an imperfect standard for determining what rivers are navigable, it nevertheless approximates the truth, and may answer very well in the Island of Great Britain, for which the rule was made. But such a standard is quite wide of the mark when applied to the great fresh water rivers of this continent, and would never have been thought of here if we had not found the rule ready made to our hands."

Senator Beardsley said, in the case of *Ex parte Tibbetts*, (5th Wendell, 423): "That the rule of the common law extending grants on the shores of rivers above the flow and re-flow of the tide, *usque filum aquæ*, does not apply to our large fresh water rivers; at all events, a patent bounded on a river navigable above tide-water passes no interest to the patentee in the bed of the river as against the State." He further remarks: "Rules of law should be adapted not only to the moral, but to the physical condition of the country. Had the common law originated on this continent, we should never have heard of the doctrine that fresh water rivers are not navigable above the flow of the tide; nor would our courts have been called upon to compromise the interests of the community by sacrificing truth to technicality, and substance to form."

This last sentence of the learned Senator, although it had reference to navigable fresh water rivers, is applicable to those decisions which hold out the idea that *all* the non-navigable salt water creeks and streams are navigable in the law.

Thurley, J., said in *Elder* v. *Burras*, (6 Humph. Tenn. 366): "All laws are or ought to be, an adaptation of the principle of action to the state and condition of a country and its moral and social position. There are many rules of action recognized in England as suitable, which it would be folly in the extreme, in countries differently located, to recognize as law; and in our opinion, this distinction between rivers navigable and not navigable, causing navigability to depend upon the ebbing and flowing of the tide, is one of them. The insular position of Great Britain, the short course of her rivers, and the well-known fact, that there are none of them navigable above tide waters, but for very small craft, well warrants the distinction there drawn by the common law."

In *McManus* v. *Carmichael* (2 Clarkes Cases in Law and Equity, Supreme Court, Iowa), Woodward, J., said: "First, Although the ebb and flow of the tide was, at common law, the most usual test of navigability, yet it was not necessarily the only one. Second, However the truth may be upon the above proposition, that the test is not applicable to the Mississippi River. Third, The common consequences of navigability attach to the legal navigability of the Mississippi." . . . . "However the truth may be upon the first proposition, the flow and re-flow of the tide is not applicable to the Mississippi, as a test of its navigability ; and the common law consequences of navigability attach to the legal navigability of the Mississippi River. The arguments and authorities on these two propositions being in a great measure identical, they must be considered together.

"The thought has been before suggested, that, as a real and virtual test, the tide is a merely arbitrary one, and is not supported by reason, since many waters where the tide flows are not in fact navigable, and many where it does not flow are so. It is navigability in fact which forms the foundation of navigability in law, and from the fact follows the appropriation to public use, and hence its publicity and legal navigability. It is true this legality attaches to some waters which do not possess the requisite quality in fact ; but this arises from their relation to the high seas and admiralty, and from the difficulty of making a hundred exceptions. It is impossible to bring the mind to an approval when we attempt to apply it to the rivers of this country, stretching three thousand miles in extent, flowing through or between independent States and bearing a commerce which competes with that of the oceans, of a test which might be applicable to an island not so large as some two of our states, and to streams whose utmost length was less than three hundred miles, and whose outlet and fountain at the same time, could be within the same State jurisdiction."

Other cases could be referred to of similar purport. But these will suffice to show how wide-spread is the opinion in the United States, that by the common law, the property of the sovereign extends to all places where the tide ebbs and flows.

It is not only remarkable that such an opinion should be so generally held, but that in one respect, the decisions all bear a family likeness. That likeness consists in that opinion being volunteered in every case so far as examined, without its having any essential connection with the question before the court. In each of these four cases, the title to the soil under fresh water rivers, which were navigable in fact, was in dispute. The preliminary question was, whether the common law was applicable to such waters, in the respective States, in which the actions were pending. It is generally conceded that by the common law, the king's title does not extend to any waters in which the tide does not ebb and flow. This is a good common law reason, because it is founded upon the fact that in England none of the rivers in their natural conditions, were actually navigable above the flow of the tide. Those parts of the rivers being incapable of any public use, no public right intervened, and consequently no right on behalf of the king attached to them. This goes to show that the king's title extends only to these waters which are actually navigable in the commercial sense, irrespective of the flow and re-flow of the tide. The question, therefore, for the court to determine in each of these cases was, not as to whether the title of the king did or did not extend to *all* waters where the tide ebbed and flowed, but whether the tide ebbed and flowed in the river in question, and that fact being ascertained, then to determine whether the river was legally navigable or not. As the tide did not flow in any of those rivers, the presumption would be that, according to the common law rule, they were not navigable. But those rivers being different in character from any in England, owing to their actual navigability, although free from the ebb and flow of the tide, that raised the very natural and pertinent question, as to whether the common law applied to such rivers or not. The common sense answer is, that it did not.

The books show comparatively few cases in which the question of the rights of property in the soil and waters of small salt water streams and creeks were involved. In only one case, as far as known, has the question as to the *prima facie* title to such a stream been openly and fairly presented and decided. That was the case of *Rowe et al.* v. *The Granite Corporation*, (21 Pick., Mass. R. 344), which will be more fully considered subsequently. In this case it was decided that such a stream was not *prima facie* presumptively a public navigable river. To raise the presumption that such waters were "navigable in fact," there must coincide, both the fact of tide and the fact of navigation being practicable. The case of *Breen* v. *Locke*, (11 N. Y. State Reporter, *supra*), involved the title to' the soil in one of the extinct Harlem Creeks. The decision in that case, in effect held that the stream was not a navigable river.

In most of the other cases the Court went out of its way to volunteer the opinion that the title to *all* streams and rivers in which the tide ebbs and flows is *prima facie* in the State or public, although that question was not before the Court for its decision.

Davies, J., in his very able and exhaustive opinion, in *The People* v. *The Canal Appraisers*, (33 N. Y. p. 461), contends that the "supposed common law doctrine," did not apply to the large fresh water rivers and lakes in New York, and further, that by the common law the term navigable river means *navigable in fact*. He says (p. 472): "While it must be conceded that Hale, in his treatise, regards it as essential to a navigable river, that it should have the ebb and flow of the tide, and ceases to be navigable in this sense, when or at the point when it is uninfluenced by the tide, yet it can not be denied that such has not been the opinion of all the English judges in all cases. Lord Mansfield correctly said *ex facto oritor jus* and it seems more rational to determine the question of navigability or un-navigability from the fact of navigation or otherwise, than from a circumstance which may or may not be conclusive evidence of its navigability.

The flow and re-flow of the tide is *prima facie* evidence as has been said, of the fact that the river *is* navigable, but the real and substantial inquiry must always be to ascertain whether the river is navigable or not. *When this main and controlling fact is established*, then we have the means of determining whether the alveus or bed of the river is the property of the adjoining owners, or belongs to the State, or the people represented by it."

The acts of the Legislature of the State of New York, relating to the grants of land under the waters or of interest in the waters of the State, show that the legal meaning of the word *navigable,* as understood by the legislature, is "navigability in fact." This application of the word navigable, in these Acts, seems to be wholly irrespective of the tide.

See Revised Laws of 1813, Vol. 1, § 4, p. 293.
R. S., Chap. 9, Title 5, Article 4, § 67.
Laws of 1850, Chap. 283, p. 621.

Some of these divergent English and American decisions will now be compared in juxtaposition.

UNITED STATES SUPPOSED COMMON LAW.

"By the term navigable river the law does not mean such as is navigable in common parlance. The smallest creek may be so to a certain extent, as well as the largest river, without being legally a navigable stream. *The term has in law a technical meaning, and applies to all streams, rivers or arms of the sea, where the tide ebbs and flows.*"

Ex parte Jennings, 6 Wend. 528, *sup.*

"It may be remarked that by the Common Law the property of the sovereign is said to extend to all places where the sea ebbs and flows, whether such *are navigable or not*; but it is probable the usages of our country have given a reasonable limitation to this doctrine, confining the public right to what may be of public use, so that in many little creeks into which the salt water flows, but which are incapable of being navigated at all, private property may be maintained."

Opinion of Parker, Ch. J., in *Commonwealth* v. *Charlestown,* 1 Pick., Mass. R. p. 179, *supra.*

ENGLISH COMMON LAW.

Lord Mansfield said: "*Ex facto oritur jus.* How does it appear that this is a navigable river? *The flowing and re-flowing of the tide does not make it so, for there are many places into which the tide flows that are not navigable rivers; and the place in question may be a creek in their own private estate.*"

Mayor of Lynn v. *Turner,* 1 Cowper, p. 86, *supra.*

"It was for the defendant to make out that there was once a public navigation. *Nor it does not necessarily follow, because the tide flows and re-flows in any particular place, that there is therefore a public navigation, although of sufficient size. The strength of this* prima facie *evidence, arising from the flux and reflux of the tide, must depend upon the situation and nature of the channel.* If it is a broad and deep channel, calculated for the purposes of commerce, it would be natural to conclude that it has been a public navigation; but if it is a petty stream, navigable only at certain periods of the tide and then only for a short time and by very small boats, it is difficult to suppose that it ever has been a public, navigable channel."

65

In the case of *Providence Steam Engine Company* v. *Providence*, 12 Rhode Island R. 348, 356, Potter, J., said: "To apply the Common Law doctrine strictly would require us to hold *that all the marshes in the State belong to the State;* yet from the very first settlement, although flowed by the tide, they have always been recognized as private property, platted and sold as such, taxed as such, and the State has made provision by statute for exempting them from the fence laws, for the very reason that they are overflowed by the tides."	Decision of Bailey, J., in *Rex* v. *Montague.* 4 B. & C. *supra*, 598. In the *De Jure Maris*, Chap. VI, there is this statement: "For such spring tides do many times overflow *ancient meadows and salt marshes, which yet unquestionably belong to the subject. And this is admitted of all hands.*"

In none of the above American cases are the statements in relation to the Common Law apparently matters of decision, but of opinion only. They should therefore be followed only in so far as they truly interpret the law. They do not profess to modify or change the law, as is the case in some of the decisions relating to the large inland rivers and lakes, but to expound and apply the law, as derived from the mother country.

There appears to be but one English decision that seems to be wholly inspired by the paragraph in the *De Jure Maris*, relating to the flow and re-flow of the tide, and it will now be considered in connection with a celebrated American decision *not* so inspired.

ENGLISH COMMON LAW DECISION.	COMMON LAW AS INTERPRETED IN THE UNITED STATES.
Trustees of Duke of Bridgewater v. *Highways of Bootle*, 7 Best & Smith's and S. C. 2, Law R. 2 B. 4.	*Esther Rowe et al.* v. *The Granite Bridge Corporation*, 21 Pick., Mass. R. 344–7. Bill in Equity.
"The Respondents, in the exercise of the powers of the general highway act (5 & 6 Wm. 4 C. 50), assessed certain parts of the Liverpool docks, in the occupation of the	"The plaintiffs allege that they are seized and possessed, as tenants in common, of a certain tract of salt marsh in Milton; that from time immemorial there has been a creek

appellants, to the highway rate of the township of Bootle, on the ground that such premises were within that township. The land upon which the docks occupied by the appellants have been constructed, was situate on the foreshore of the river Mersey, between the ordinary or medium high water and low water mark, but the land has been re-claimed, and the tide no longer flows over it. Before the construction of these docks, the township of Bootle extended on its western side, along part of its course as far as the sea, and along other parts as far as the mouth of the river Mersey. There was nothing to show whether the Township of Bootle along its western side, does or does not extend beyond the line of the ordinary high water mark, and if necessary for the purpose of the case, the Court were to decide what is the western boundary of the Township."

Mellor, J., said: "There must be judgment for the appellant. The respondents have to show that the premises they have rated are within their township. Now, in the absence of any evidence, such as perambulation or other acts by the parish authorities, the land between medium high water and low water mark cannot be presumed to be within the adjoining parish; the presumption seems rather to be that it is extra parochial and here there is no evidence on the point. I can not help thinking there must be some misapprehension in the report of *Rex* v. *Landulph*, as what is attributed to Patterson, J., seems quite inapplicable to the circumstances of the case; at all events the ruling as reported is inconsistent with the authorities on the point, for there seems to be no distinction between commencing at the high part of the marsh, and passing through it to Nepnotes River, whereby the tidewater is drained off from the marsh, which creek is of sufficient width and depth to admit boats and gondolas and light-draft craft to pass up the creek in common tides, and such craft may be used to advantage in removing the crops of hay from the marsh; that the defendants, by their act of incorporation, were authorized to construct a road over the lands therein mentioned and to build a bridge over the Neponset River; that pursuant to their authority they had laid out the road over the marsh and across the creek, and as the creek runs in an angular direction to that in which the road is laid out, the road passes over the creek the distance of fifteen rods, . . . and that the defendants are proceeding to fill up the creek; and the bill prays for an injunction," etc.

Shaw, Ch. J., delivered the opinion of the Court. He said: "This is a bill in equity, which comes before the Court upon regular pleadings and proofs. It goes substantially upon the ground of nuisance, and prays for a perpetual injunction against the defendants. . . . . But the question which has been mainly discussed in the present case is: *Whether the creek in question is a navigable creek; and this is a question of fact upon the evidence*. Before examining this evidence it may be proper to consider what distinctly is meant by a *navigable stream when applied to tide-water. It is not every ditch in which the salt water ebbs and flows* through the extensive salt marshes along the coast, and which serve to admit and drain off the salt water from the marshes, which can be considered a navigable stream.

the seashore and the shore of a tidal river. There is no foundation for this rating, either on the above principle or on the construction of the Highway Act; and the respondents having failed to make out any *prima facie* right to rate the dock, the other questions are immaterial, and there must be judgment for the appellants."

Shea, J. and Lush, J. concurred.

Having in view the above English authorities, it will hardly seem presumptious to say that if anybody was mistaken it was not Patterson, J., but rather Mellor, J.

It is as plain as the proposition that two and two make four, that any one who lays claim to a piece of land below high water mark in a place like the harbor of Liverpool, must prove title, or be defeated. It was not, therefore, necessary for the Court to express an opinion whether the judgment in *Rex* v. *Laneulph* was sound or not. Mellish, Q. C., for appellant, relied mainly upon the ebb and flow passage in the *De Jure Maris*, and evidently carried the Court with him, for it not only adopted his views, but his very language.

By this decision the Duke of Bridgewater's estate escaped taxation under a technicality. Whether it could be taxed by anybody, quere?

Nor is it every creek in which a fishing skiff or gunning canoe can be made to float at high water, which is deemed to be navigable. But in order to have this character it must be navigable to some purpose useful to trade or agriculture. *It is not a mere possibility of being used under some circumstances, as at extraordinary tides which will give it the character of a navigable stream. But it must be generally and commonly useful to some purpose of trade and agriculture.*"

In the case of *The Montello*, 20 Wallace, 430 U. S. Rep., Davis, Justice, cites with approval the above decision of Ch. J. Shaw, quoting his language relating to the fishing skiff, etc. He then says: "This Court, in the case of the *Daniel Ball* (10 Wall.) held, that those rivers must be regarded as navigable rivers in law, which are navigable in fact. And they are navigable in fact when they are used, or are susceptible of being used, in their ordinary conditions as highways of commerce over which trade and travel are or may be conducted in the customary modes of trade or travel on water."

This definition is quite in harmony with that given by Lord Denman in *Colchester* v. *Brooke* (*supra*).

Let these decisions be tested in the light of the rule laid down by Blackstone : " But here a very natural and very material question arises, how are these customs or maxims to be known, and by whom is their validity to be determined ? The answer is, by the judges in the several Courts of justice. They are the depositories of the laws, the living oracles, who must decide in all cases of doubt, and who are bound by an oath to decide according to the law of the land. Their knowledge of that law is derived from experience and study; from the *viginti annorum lucubrationes* which Fortescue mentions; and from being long personally accustomed to the judicial decisions of their predecessors. And *indeed* these judicial decisions are the principal and most authoritative evidence that can be given of the existence of such a custom as shall form part of the common law. The judgment itself, and all the proceedings previous thereto, are carefully registered and preserved, under the name of records, in public depositories set apart for that particular purpose, and to them frequent recourse is had when any critical question arises, in the determination of which former precedents may give light or assistance. . . . For it is an established rule to abide by former precedents, where the same points come up again in litigation, as well to keep the scale of justice even and steady and not liable to waver with every new judge's opinion; as also because the law in that case being solemnly declared and determined, what before was uncertain, and perhaps indifferent, is now become a permanent rule which it is not in the breast of any subsequent judge to alter or vary from according to his own private sentiments, he being sworn to determine, not according to his own private judgment, but according to the known laws and customs of the land; not delegated to pronounce a new law, but to maintain and expound the old one. Yet this rule admits of exception, where the former determination is most evidently contrary to reason—much more if it be clearly contrary to the divine law. But even in such cases the subsequent judges do not pretend to make a new law, but to vindicate the old one from misrepresentation. For if it be found that the former decision is manifestly absurd and unjust, it is declared, not that such a sentence was *bad law*, but that it was *not law;* that is, that it is not the established custom of the realm, as has been erroneously determined."

Blackstone's Com., V. 1, p. 69.

And at p. 71 he further says: "So that *the law* and the *opinion of the judge* are not always convertible terms, or one and the same thing; since it sometimes may happen that the judge may *mistake* the law.

By the common law there are three kinds of rivers. First; "Navigable rivers, so high as the sea ebbs and flows," which are also denominated "royal rivers." Second; other tidal rivers "not navigable." Third; "Inland rivers not navigable."

Gould, *supra*, p. 107, note 1.

These rivers are divided into two classes, public and private rivers. The royal rivers are the public rivers, because they "are of common or public use for the carriage of boats and lighters, and common highways for man and for goods." The other rivers, whether fresh or salt, "are private not only in propriety or ownership, but also in use." These are private, because in their natural conditions they are not suitable for commerce, and are therefore not required by the people.

De Jure Maris, c. 3.

If a grant is made by the Government of land bordering upon a public navigable river to a private person or corporation, it extends only to the medium high water line. If such a grant is made to a municipal or civil corporation for public purposes, it goes to the low water mark.

The Mayor, &c., of New York v. *Hart*, 95 N. Y. p. 450.
Rogers v. *Jones*, 1 Wend. 238, *supra*.

If a grant is made by the Government or a private person of land bordering on a stream either of fresh or salt water and the same is not navigable, in fact, the grant extends to the center of the stream. See cases above cited.

This rule is in accordance with the principles embraced in the decision in *ex parte*, Jennings, *supra*, and the other following cases. In *Ex parte*, Jennings, the question was the construction of a grant made by the State of lands bordering on the Chittenango Creek. Jennings claimed to be the owner of the bed of the creek. The Supreme Court held that the Chittenango Creek was not navigable, because the tide did not ebb and flow in it. It decided that grants included the stream. The Court said: "If the State had intended to retain the property in the stream, they should have inserted an express reservation or exception to their grants. An opposite rule prevails in the construction of grants bounded on the margin of navigable rivers." (Then follows the opinion as to what constitutes a navigable river, above quoted). "A public grant bounded upon the margin of such waters extends by construction no further than high water mark, and leaves as to the rest, an absolute propriety interest in the public."

In *Child* v. *Starr*, 4 Hill, the case involved the title to part of the Genessee River, Bradish, President, in delivering the opinion, said (p. 380): "Though the term *shore* is technically applicable only to the sea, to lakes or to other large bodies of water, yet in its judicial and popular application to rivers, it is, by elementary writers, the adjudications of the Courts and in common understanding, as clearly defined, as well settled, and as universally recognized, as is the *filum aquae*, or thread of the stream, and a grant of land bounded generally on or running along *a private stream*, would not more certainly carry the grant to the thread of the stream, than would a grant bounded by and running along the *shore* of such a stream, be limited to the waters edge or margin of the stream."

In this case, Walworth, Chan. said (pp. 373, 375): "The Common Law rule, as I understand it, is that the riparian proprietor is *prima facie* the owner of the *alveus* or bed of the river adjoining his land, to the middle or thread of the stream; that is, where the terms of his grant do not appear to show that he is limited.

And when by the terms of the grant to the riparian proprietor he is bounded upon the river generally, as a natural boundary, or in the language of Pothier, where the grant to the riparian proprietor has no other boundary on the side thereof, which is adjacent to the river, but the stream itself, the legal presumption is that his grantor intended to convey to the middle of the stream, subject to the right of the public to use the waters of the river for the purposes of navigation in their accustomed channel."

This is Chancellor Kent's statement of the rights of riparian proprietors: "It is a settled principle of the English law, that rights of soil, of owners of land bounded by the sea, or *navigable rivers where the tide ebbs and flows* extend to high water mark; and the shore below common, but not extraordinary high water mark belongs to the State as trustee for the public; and in England the Crown, and in this country the people, have the absolute proprietory interest in the same, though it may by grant or prescription become private property. . . . . But the shores of navigable waters, and the soil under them belong to the State in which they are situated, are sovereign. The right of sovereignty in public rivers above the flow of the tide is the same as in tide-waters, they are *juris publici*, except that the proprietors adjoining such rivers, own the soil *ad filum aquæ*. But grants of land bounded on rivers or upon the margins of the same, or along the same, above tide-water carry the exclusive right and title of the grantee to the centre of the stream, unless the terms of the grant clearly denote the intention to stop at the edge or margin of the river; and the public in cases where the river is navigable for boats and rafts, have an easement thereon or right of passage subject to the *jus publicum* as a public highway. The proprietors of the adjoining banks have a right to use the river as regards the public."

Kent's Com., Vol. 3, p. 427, m. p.

This statement is evidently drawn in the main from the treatise *De Jure Maris*. So far as it goes, it is in entire agreement with the English authorities. It does not define what a navigable river is, further than that it must be tidal. It does not lay down the iron rule, that every stream where the tide ebbs and flows, even "*to the smallest creek*," is a *navigable river*.

It is true that he did not make so comprehensive a definition as Lord Hale. He did not state that, not only must the tide ebb and flow in a navigable river, but that it must be "of common and public use, for the carriage of boats and lighters, and a common highway for man or for goods, or for both." And he did not include all the "streams or rivers that are private not only in proprietory or ownership, but also in use, as little streams and rivers that are not a common passage for the king's people," but only referred to those streams of that character, that are above the ebb and flow of the tide. He makes no reference to small tidal creeks either directly or by implication. Neither does he go into the question of public use as the preliminary test of a navigable river, as seems to be the case in all the English enquires, where the river is not of such a public notoriety, as to be legally known to be a navigable river.

In a recent action in ejectment brought by *Edward Roberts* v. *August Baumgarten, et al* (51 N. Y. Supr. Court, p. 482), the plaintiff claimed title to part of the bed of Harlem Mill Creek. He founded his claim upon a title derived through a deed made by Benjamin Benson to his son Peter B. Benson, in 1791, conveying as follows: "All that messuage or tenement, being all my estate to the North of the Mill Pond, between the fence of the widow Storm, and the road leading to Harlem, including the Mill Stream and Mill and Mill Pond, with all its privileges and appurtenances, and to shut the mill dam at the South side of said Mill Pond, where it now lays." (This deed is examined and construed *post*.) On the trial the plaintiff attempted to prove title to the creek east of the dam, but failed.

The answer was a general denial and allegation of title and possession of the premises in dispute.

On the trial the plaintiff produced as a witness S., who testified that he was a City Surveyor. That as such he had charge of the work of grading Second Avenue across this creek about thirty years before. That at Second Avenue, when he graded it there was at low tide one or two feet of water, and at high tide about eight feet. That he could not say that the creek was navigable. That they used to bring up scows and such boats in the creeek, that he could not say that he ever saw them up as far as the Third Avenue. That the tide ebbed and flowed in the creek.

On the defense B. was examined as a witness, and testified that he was familiar with the property in dispute and that neighborhood, and had known it for forty-three years.

That the creek was navigable at high tide up to within a few feet of Third Avenue; that he had often seen sloops and canal boats there loaded with material. That he did not know whether the creek was wide enough for two of such boats to pass each other going up and down, that he did not know that he ever saw two or three in the creek at once, that there was very little water in the stream in some places at low tide, that he could not tell whether the stream was 80 or 100 feet wide, that it was very deceptive looking at water, that there were no docks in that neighborhood, that he did not know the height of the tide or amount of water, that his observation was that of a casual observer, that he had seen vessels passing up and down, boats and sailing vessels, loaded with cargoes of brick and lime, such as small sloops, that he never saw a schooner or steamboat in the creek.

The learned trial judge rested his decision solely on the deed from Benjamin Benson to Peter B. Benson, by which he held that Peter B. Benson and those claiming under him became vested with the title and possession of the premises mentioned in the deed, and gave judgment for the plaintiff from which the defendant appealed to the General Term.

See this deed examined and construed, *post*. See printed case on appeal to the General Term.

This evidence as to the character of the creek and its use for commercial purposes was not sufficient under the common law rule, to show a public navigation.

See cases cited, *supra*.

In this case the question of its navigability was not *res judicatæ*.

Sedgwick, Ch. J., in delivering the opinion of the Court, O'Gorman, J., and Ingraham J., concurring, said: " I am further of the opinion that the deed on which the plaintiff relies for proof of title (*i. e.*, Benjamin Benson to Peter B. Benson) does not describe the land between high and low water mark on Harlem Creek between the dam and the river." . . . . " In this case Benson (Peter B.) owned no part of the land under the stream formed by the creek East of the dam. It should not for that reason be inferred, that the description was intended to convey more than it would if he had been or claimed to be owner of some of the land."

This case merely decides that Peter B. Benson and those claiming under him from the deed produced in evidence had no title to the premises in dispute (which lay South of the middle line of the creek, East of the mill dam, part being above and part below high water mark.) This is all that it was necessary to decide in order to dispose of the plaintiff's claim.

In the beginning of his opinion the learned Justice makes this statement. "The creek was a small body of water *that may be called* an arm of the Harlem River. As the tide ebbed and flowed in it, the presumption would be that the stream was navigable *People* v. *Canal Appraisers*, (33 N. Y., 472, opinion of Judge Davies). In this case its un-navigability was to be proved by the plaintiff. It is clear that the facts tended to show navigability in fact. The title to the land in question was then in the State or public, or in the City of New York *Mayor* v. *Hart*, (95 N. Y., 443). No conveyance appears to have been made by the City or the State. It therefore appears that the grantors in the deed from Johnson to Benjamin Benson, and from Benjamin Benson to Peter B. Benson had no title, nor by presumption or actual possession."

It is to be noted that the question as to whether this creek was an arm of the Harlem River or not, was not before the Court. Neither was the question of the title to it. The court does not decide that the creek was in fact an arm of the Harlem River, but merely states that "it may be *called an arm* of the Harlem River." Strictly speaking it was a fresh water stream or rivulet, which emptied into the Harlem River, the waters of which were backed up for a considerable distance by the flood tides of the river.

It was not therefore an integral part of the river.

See *Breen* v. *Locke*, 11 N. Y. State Reporter, p. 288.

The facts in regard to the creek which was the subject of the controversy in *Breen* v. *Locke*, were almost identical with those relating to Harlem Creek. An inspection of the topographical maps of Randall, Coulton (1836), or Viele will show this. Both creeks " were created partly by several water streams when descending from the water shed of the high ground in the neighbourhood, and partly by the waters of the Harlem River." In both cases there was very little water in the creeks at low tide. In both cases the creeks were navigable for small vessels at high tide. " There was nothing cove-like in either of the creeks, even when the tide in them was high." In both cases the premises were between high and low water mark. The shore contours of both were those of a widened stream. In both cases the creeks have been filled up and avenues and streets constructed over parts of the ground they occupied.

The creek at Eighth Avenue and 155th Street was probably more than twice as wide as Harlem Creek. The direct question which the Court was called upon to decide in *Breen* v. *Locke* was, as to whether the bed of the creek belonged to the City of New York, or the Town of Harlem. The case turned upon the construction of the Harlem patents, and the reasoning of the Court seems to be conclusive.

Bartlett, J., says: "An inspection of the topographical map between pp. 39 and 40 of the printed case goes very far towards satisfying us on this point.

"It would seem very inaccurate for any one using language in its ordinary sense, to speak of the premises, as shown on that map, as being situated on the Harlem River, or any part of it. Naturally a person endeavoring to describe their location in general terms, would say they were partly in the bed and partly on the shore, between high and low water mark of a creek leading into the Harlem River. There was nothing cove-like about the creek, even when the tide in it was high. The shore contours were those of a widened stream. The land in dispute was 898 feet from the main body of the Harlem River at high tide.

"It is difficult to perceive how the creek at this point could be of any value or importance to the City of New York in a commercial sense. 'The City was to be the seaport,' says the Court of Appeals in the case of *The Mayor, &c.* v. *Hart, supra,* and for this purpose *its water front was to girdle the whole island,* while the village (of Harlem) was meant for a rustic hamlet, whose inhabitants should own cattle rather than ships.

"But it does not seem to us that the portion of this creek, upon which these premises were located, constituted any part of the water front thus spoken of in that case. The fact that the creek there has been filled up and that a part of it is covered by the road bed of the Eighth Avenue, is pretty conclusive evidence that it was valueless for any use connected with shipping.

"As to this fundamental objection to the title then, our conclusion is, that the land in question was conveyed to the freeholders and inhabitants of Harlem by the patents already mentioned, and that the title thereto did not pass to the City of New York under the Dongan Charter."

The judgment in *Breen* v. *Locke,* rests upon the decision in *Mayor, &c.* v. *Hart.* The language of the Court of Appeals in that case is, that under the Dongan Charter the City of New York acquired the title to the tide-way or land between high and low water mark on the *whole circiut* of Manhattan Island, p. 450. Again on page 452: 'We are satisfied that the *River line* was the high water mark, and so the City owned the tide-way."

In *Roberts* v. *Baumgarten* the Harlem patents were not produced in evidence, and not referred to in the decision, and it may be assumed that they were not taken into consideration in forming the judgment. This is rendered the more probable from the fact, that while Justice O'Gorman was Corporation Counsel for New York, he furnished the Comptroller with an opinion relative to the McGown marshes, in which he arrived at the conclusion, that the City did not acquire any title in the marshes by virtue of the Dongan Charter. The reasoning embodied in this opinion would lead irresistibly to the conclusion that the Harlem creeks passed also to the freeholders and inhabitants of Harlem under their patents.

See opinion of Judge O'Gorman, Appendix D.

Neither was the deed from Director Kieft and his Council to Dr. John Montagne, nor the deed from the Town of Harlem to John Montagne the younger (*supra*) put in evidence on the trial of that case, so that the question of the title to the Harlem Mill Creek, as derived under those patents, and the title to the southerly half of that creek and mill pond as conveyed by those deeds, had not been before the Court.

The judgment of the General Term reversing the judgment at Special Term in the case of *Roberts* v. *Baumgarten* was affirmed by the Court of Appeals, October 2, 1888 (110 N. Y., p. 380). Gray, J., in delivering the opinion, said: "The plaintiff claims to derive his title through *mesne* conveyances, from one Benjamin Benson. Benjamin Benson's deed to Peter B. Benson, his son, *which was relied upon by the plaintiff* as a source of title, conveyed by the following description, viz. . . . "Under this description plaintiff claims that the whole of Harlem Mill Creek, between the tops of its banks, was conveyed, and that the grantee acquired the ownership of the bed of that stream. Such a construction of the grant, however, is not permissible, either by well settled rules of law, or in the light which the facts, disclosed by the proofs, throw upon the claim. Harlem creek was subject to ebb and flow of the tide to a point beyond the premises in question. Such bodies of water, at common law, were deemed to be navigable, and held to be royal rivers, or the property of the Crown. They were placed on the same footing as the sea, and regarded as public highways. This rule of the common law became a part of the fundamental law of this State, by the adoption of the original constitution of 1777. There have been no revisions of that instrument or any acts of the Legislature which in any wise affected the continuance of such a rule as part of the body of the law of our State, and as one which governs in cases where the rights of riparian owners to waters subject to tidal influences are in question. To the rights of the Crown the people in this State succeeded upon their separation, and the title to the lands under water, where the tide flows and re-flows, vested and remained in them. This rule has been uniformly recognized in the adjudged cases in the reports of this State which discuss the title of the people in such lands."

As has been before remarked, the decision in this case rested on the issue raised in the pleading, namely : the construction of the deed by Benjamin Benson to Peter B. Benson. The learned judge's statements in regard to the common law of England on tidal waters are, of course, entitled to respectful and thoughtful consideration; but if these statements are not of the substance of the judgment, the rule laid down by the great jurist, Blackstone, above quoted, is still open to us for application to the case now under examination.

It is noteworthy, that both the General Term decision and that of the Court of Appeals refer to the case of *The People* v. *The Canal Appraisers* (33 N. Y. 461), and yet an examination of that case will fail to show *any decision* which in express terms holds that by the Common Law of England the title of the Crown extended to *all* waters where the tide ebbs and flows, irrespective of whether such waters are in fact navigable or not. It is believed that question has never been squarely presented and adjudicated upon in any court of final resort in this State. It is very difficult to bring the mind to believe that if the question could be fairly and fully presented to the Court of Appeals, by an intelligent presentation of the case, that that Court would render a decision holding that : "*By the term navigable river, the law does not mean such as is navigable in common parlance. The smallest creek may be so to a certain extent, as well as the largest river, without being legally a navigable stream. The term has in law a technical meaning, and applies to all streams, rivers, and arms of the sea where the tide ebbs and flows.*"

Vide *Ex parte* Jennings.

But we are bound to concede that when a question of law is fully and fairly presented to the Court of Appeals, with such assistance as learned counsel can render for the information of the Court, that this august tribunal, in its collective wisdom, will beyond doubt, render a decision in accordance with the law.

Some well-known facts appear to have been not brought to the attention of the learned judges who delivered the opinions of the General Term and the Court of Appeals, namely: That for many years the briny waters of the East River had ceased to make their diurnal journeys up and down the grassy channel of Harlem Mill Creek; that for more than thirty years that creek had ceased to receive the visits of the fishing skiff, the gunning canoe, the awkward scow, or the picturesque sloop; that during that time it had ceased to be a royal or any other kind of fishery; that the finny tribes, including the bass, flounder, and slippery eel, had wholly disappeared from its romantic waters; that the soft and yielding channel of that ancient stream was no longer occupied by grasses, mosses, and aquatic plants, but that they had been supplanted, and its beautiful channel filled up to the very brim and over by ashes, garbage, dirt and rubbish—the conventional filling supplied by the street contractor in lieu of the "good and wholesome earth" required by law.

What the learned judge says in delivering the opinion of the Court of Appeals as to the present binding force of the Common Law, as recognized by the Constitution of 1777, is unanswerable. By that standard must this question be determined, and not by any opinions which are deviations from that law.

Let us now examine an English case, quite similar in its nature. The case of *Rex* v. *Montague* (4 B. & C. 598, *supra*.) was an indictment for cutting a trench across a common and ancient highway. At the trial it appeared that the highway in question was an embankment across a creek, and that the defendants cut down this embankment by order of the Corporation of London, who contended that the creek was a public navigable stream and that the road improperly obstructed it; that the road had been so high for twenty years that no boats could pass over it at any time; that for years before, the only evidence of an actual navigation was by very small boats for a brief period at the time of high water.

Notwithstanding the proof that this was *a tidal creek*, the court held that: "It was for the *defendant* to make out that there was once a public navigation." If, according to the Common Law, *all creeks* in which the tide ebbed and flowed "were deemed to be navigable, and held to be royal rivers, or the property of the Crown," as Judge Gray expresses it, then this English decision is wrong. The Court should have said in regard to the creek, as the tide ebbed and flowed in it, the presumption would be that the stream was navigable. In this case its un-navigability was to be proved by the plaintiff (opinion of Sedgwick, Ch. J.): *i. e.*, the party who constructed the trench across the creek, and not the defendant, City of London, which removed the obstruction.

Bailey, J., in delivering the opinion, goes on to say: "But even supposing this to have been at some time a public navigation, I think that from the manner in which it has been neglected by the public, and from the length of time during which it has been obstructed, it ought to be presumed that the rights of the public have been lawfully determined. . . . But they might have been put an end to by act of Parliament, or by writ *ad quod damnum*, and perhaps by commissioners of sewers, if there were any appointed for the district and they found that it would be for the benefit of the whole level.

"For these reasons it appears to me that if this case were sent down for trial again, the jury would be bound to find either that there never was a public navigation through the *locus in quo*, or it has been determined by some lawful means."

And after reviewing the cases of *Mayor of Lynn* v. *Turner* and *Miles* v. *Rose, supra*, he said: "The strength of this *prima facie* evidence, arising from the flux and reflux of the tide must depend upon the situation and nature of the channel," etc.

Holroyd, J., and Littledale, J., gave opinions to the same effect. Now it is to be noted that this case not only cites with approval the case of *Mayor of Lynn* v. *Turner*, but uses almost the identical language of Lord Mansfield in that case.

In *Roberts* v. *Baumgarten*, although the important fact was before the court that the City of New York, acting under the authority of the Legislature, had actually closed this creek thirty years before the trial, and destroyed whatever navigable capacity it had, it seems to have been overlooked or considered immaterial.

The Second Avenue was established by law across this creek as far back as 1837, by proceeding for opening that avenue, and the bed of that part of the creek was taken by the commissioners and the title acquired by the City for a public avenue. Of these proceedings the Court, probably, had judicial notice. These facts raised the presumption, that the creek was not a public stream according to the law as laid down in *Rex* v. *Montague, supra*. As that is a common law decision of acknowledged authority, it ought to control in *Roberts* v. *Baumgarten*, not only as to the creek, being a private stream because of its obliteration, but also on account of its location, small size, and failure of adequate proof that it had been used as a public navigable channel, time out of mind.

The deed on which the plaintiff relied, clearly did not include the *locus in quo*, and to remedy that defect in his claim the plaintiff attempted to prove title by prescription, to that part of the creek, on which to found the claim that his grant properly interpreted, included the premises in question. To meet this, the defendant attempted to show that the creek was a public navigable stream. The defendant's counsel was evidently aware that proof that the tide ebbed and flowed in the creek was not of itself sufficient to establish that fact, but was only one of the elements going to show it, and that in addition, he must show an actual public navigation and of sufficient length of time to bring it within the requirements of the law.

The plaintiff also failed to show title by prescription to

any part of the premises claimed by him, and this really disposed of the plaintiff's claim. But as the question of the navigability of this creek was raised in this case, although that question was not material, under the evidence presented by the plaintiff, the evidence offered by the defendant was not sufficient to establish the fact that this was a public navigable stream.

In *Vooght* v. *Winch* (2 B. & A. 662 *supra*), the learned judge who tried the cause declined to allow the question to go to the jury on the evidence, to consider whether the stream called Channel Sea River was navigable, and *in what way*, whether as *a public* navigable river, *or for the convenience of the adjoining occupiers;* "even although it had been a public navigable river," and he further added, that whether navigable or not, he thought the party was bound to use the water in the state in which it was found to be for the space of twenty years invariably, and that a benefit so long enjoyed could not afterwards be disturbed.

It is true that on the appeal of this case the appellate Court held that it was error in not allowing the case to go to the jury, to say whether the stream was ever a public navigable stream or not; but in other respects the judgment does not seem to have been disturbed.

In the case of *Roberts* v. *Baumgarten*, the defendant's testimony entirely failed to come up to the requirements of the law as laid down in *Vooght* v. *Winch*. It did not show twenty years use of the water, nor even that the use of the water as proved by the defendant, was not for the convenience of the adjoining owners on each side of the creek. This might have been the case, and therefore there was a failure to show any use by the public. Aside from this, the fact that the tide ebbed and flowed in the creek did not of itself raise the presumption that there was, therefore, a public navigation, although the channel may have been of sufficient size.

Besides it was in evidence that this creek was closed by virtue of an act of the Legislature, more than thirty years before, and the rights of the public, if it ever had any, have been thereby lawfully determined.

To hold that in *all* tidal waters, according to the common law, the title to the bed of the stream is *prima facie* in the crown, would unsettle the titles to those minor creeks and private navigable rivers which time out of mind have belonged to the subject, to say nothing of the numerous little creeks which flow through the marshes, which have always belonged, *prima facie*, to the subject.

Mayor of Lynn v. *Turner* (1 Cowper, p. 86).
Rex v. *Montague* (4 B. & C. 598).
De Jure Maris, C. 6.
Providence Steam Engine Co. v. *Providence* (12 R. I. 348-356 *supra*).

To return to the creeks which are the subject of this inquiry. There was nothing in regard to them calculated to raise the presumption that they were in any respect public waters.

"They had no *caput portus*, for the receipt of mariners and merchants, and the securing and vending of goods and victualling their ships." Neither were they directly or remotely connected with such a port or with navigation in any way. As has been before remarked they ran through marshes, so far as the water was salt. At the spring tides they overflowed their banks, and submerged the surrounding flats to a considerable extent. They were not arms of the sea in any true and proper sense of the term. They were located in a somewhat barren, and wholly unpopulated region of country. The object of the grants of lands bordering on the streams was to encourage the establishment of farms. There seems to be no reliable authority, or logical or common sense reason, for limiting these grants to the line of high water mark, that would not apply with equal force, if the creeks had been wholly of fresh water. That being the case, the grants extended to the *filum aquae* of the respective creeks. The above authorities appear to show very clearly that, according to the Common Law, small creeks and streams like those mentioned in the deed from Director-General Kieft and his council to Dr. Johannes Montagne, were not public, but were *prima facie* private waters. Rivulets of that character were a distinguishing feature of Manhattan Island. From the high ground which ranged along the center of the island for almost its entire length, and which was ultimately known as "The Backbone of the Island," innumerable springs of pure water flowed East, West and North, and emptied into the East and North Rivers, and Harlem Kills and Spuyten Duyvel Creek. Into the mouths of all these creeks the tide ebbed and flowed. Many of the streams were of considerable size and capable of forming harbors for sloops and other vessels. All these creeks (with two or three exceptions in the Harlem River) have disappeared and given place to the thoroughfares and solid structures of this great Metropolis. One of these streams issued from the Collect Pond and flowed through a marsh Northwesterly, substantially along the line of Canal Street to the North River. A stone bridge crossed the stream at Broadway in the early part of this century. Another stream flowed Southeasterly and emptied into the East River at about the foot of James Street.

It is a matter of tradition, if not of history, that at one time it was in contemplation to construct a canal through the marshes, and about on the line of Canal Street, to connect the Hudson River with the Collect Pond; the canal to be used for the passage of vessels to and from the river to that pond, and to locate the public market on the margin of the pond.

The question naturally arises as to why all these creeks were closed and filled up, if the parts in which the tide ebbed and flowed were public navigable waters and highways of commerce. If, in the early days of the history of Manhattan Island, the navigable portions of these small streams were not considered to be of sufficient value to be kept open for public use, of how much less importance do they appear at the present time? In these days of immense steam and sailing ships, of four masted schooners, of yachts rivaling in tonnage an ancient man-of-war, of railways crossing broad rivers, almost trackless marshes and passing through great mountains, it appears to be very unreasonable to talk of little streams like those mentioned in the Montagne deed, being public navigable waters.

The existence of a structure like the Brooklyn Bridge testifies to the fact that even commerce must yield up some of its privileges and prerogatives to the requirements of modern progress. The Harlem patents included all the right and title of the Sovereign to the creeks and watercourses with the soil under them, within the bounds of the lands granted, without any reservation. This of itself raises the presumption that the creeks were not public, navigable waters.

CHAPTER IX.
The McGown Marshes, or the Meadows in the Bay of Hellgate.

The early history of part of these meadows is related in Chapter V. *ante*. Subsequently to the arrangement with Director Stuyvesant, by which John Montagne the younger retained Montagne's Point as part of his father's estate, and before he obtained the deed for the same from the authorities of the town of Harlem, as related in that chapter, he made an exchange of a parcel of meadow land "lying south of the Great Meadow" for the Meadows in the Bay of Hellgate. These meadows, together with those belonging to Montagne's Point, constituted the McGown Marshes.

Before continuing the history of this title, a brief account will be given of the Harlem Marshes.

The ample fertile plains, the salt marshes and intersecting creeks, and the springs and fresh-water stream were the attractions which led to the early settlements in Harlem. That the salt marshes were highly prized from the beginning is shown by the historical records. In the early days, such of the meadows as were not granted or alloted were used in common. A few extracts are given by way of illustration. The first is:—An Order issued by Governor Nicholls, prior to granting his second patent:

"A warrant to the constable of Westchester about some Meadow Ground claimed by Harlem.

"Whereas, I am informed that the *Inhabitants of Harlem have for divers years mowed their hay* in the meadows on the other side of Harlem River, where John Archer of your town pretends an interest by virtue of a patent granted for the Yonker's Land to Hugh O'Neale and Mary his wife. These are, to require you to warn the said John Archer, that he forbear cutting hay in those Meadows this present season, and likewise that he do not presume to molest those of Harlem until I shall be fully satisfied *of the Titles* on both parts, and give my judgment thereupon to whom of right these Meadows do belong.

"Given under my hand at Fort James, in New York, this 16th day of August, 1667." "R. NICOLLS."

These were the meadows, lots 1, 2, 3, 4, "over against the Spring" on the northerly shore of the Harlem River. It was the omission of these lots, together with the meadow lots 1, 2, 3, 4, "going through Bronk's Kill over against Great Barne's Island," from the patent, as well as the change of the name of the town, which gave so much dissatisfaction with that patent. The fact that the disputed meadows were included in the Second Patent shows that the Governor decided in favor of Harlem. The Order of the Dutch Director and Council provided "that for each 18 to 24 *morgen* of arable land there should be allowed six or eight *morgen* of meadow."

As to Little Barent's Island, Stuyvesant had granted the meadows lying around it to some of the Harlem People, and had allowed all of them to use the Island for the pasturing their young stock.

Delavall's meadows on this island lay in common with Cresson's, and Cresson was willing to give up his part, provided he could have the meadow west of the Hills along Montagne's Kill, *at the north side of the Kill*, and if the person using Barent's Island would help him a day in making fence.

Riker's Hist., p. 264.

The Round Meadow named in the patent was called Moertje David's Vly, or Mother David's Meadow. It was the identical meadow named in Kuyter's grant, and lay just within the Bay, or close at Manhattanville, and it was so named to distinguish it from another "Round Meadow" at Sherman's Creek, called in the original allotments the Great Meadow.

Riker's Hist., pp. 146, 192, 27, 272, 264, 261.

"The farmers used a 'Wey-schuyt' (boat) to bring their hay from the meadows."

In the bay formed by Hoorn's Hook and Rechawanes, or Montagne's Point, as it was subsequently called, and the high rocky hills at the south and west, there was at the time of the grants to Huddie and Montagne a series of these meadows. They ranged mostly, easterly from Third Avenue, and the exterior easterly points extended to about Avenue "A." The deepest part of the bay was at 98th Street, and there for a short distance the margin was a little west of the westerly side of First Avenue. At this point a broad creek led through the meadows, crossing Second Avenue at 99th Street; thence in a northwesterly direction to a point a little north of 100th Street, and easterly from Third Avenue, and thence northeasterly and northwesterly to a point between 103d and 104th Streets and Fourth and Lexington Avenues, where it formed the outlet for a brook which had its source in the high grounds now in Central Park.

There were a number of small creeks intersecting these meadows. The large creek divided the range into two parts. The northerly and greater portion was attached to Montagne's Point; the remainder of the range, lying southerly of the division creek, was known as The Meadows in the Bay of Hellgate. This name was no doubt given because at this point the bay had its greatest depression and lay directly opposite the perturbed waters of Hellgate. While the outlines of the bay have been somewhat changed by the construction of bulkheads or slips in some places, or solid filling, the meadows have disappeared and given place to avenues and streets, and to a considerable extent to substantial buildings. There is, however, a small section still remaining, which may be seen on the shore of the Harlem River between 103d and 104th Streets, near the projected line of Avenue A. A creek divides the meadows, into which the tide ebbs and flows as of old.

See Map, Appendix I, showing the meadows and Montague's Point.

It is generally, but erroneously supposed, that all of the meadows lying between Hoorn's Hook and Montagne's Point were included under the general designation of the Meadows in the Bay of Hellgate. The proper classification of these two parcels should be kept in mind. The northerly portion formed part of the original Harlem Farm settled upon by Hendrick de Forest, granted by ground brief to Huddie, and purchased by Dr. de La Montagne at the auction sale at Fort Amsterdam, and expressly mentioned in the description in the deed to him in which the Point is described as being *between two kills*. The title to the northern division of these meadows, therefore, has its source in the first ground brief granted for any land in Harlem. All the marsh land included between the division creek and the high land of Montagne's Point became absolutely vested under the grants to Huddie and Montagne long before the advent of the English or the granting of any of the patents and charters by the British governors. This land also has the further distinction of being a part of the land that was first sold by order of the Court on Manhattan Island; and what title can possibly be better than a "*Court title?*"

It is quite probable that the southerly portion of these meadows was allotted to the Dutch Church in Harlem prior to the British occupation, as may be inferred from the following historical statements of Riker, p. 192, &c.:—

"Salt hay was thought indispensable for the cattle; hence a small parcel of marsh or meadow, usually about three *morgen*, was set off to each lot of bouwland. That all might be supplied, these had to be taken wherever found on Little Barent's and Stony Island, on the other side of Harlem River, about Spuyten Duyvel, and in the Great Meadow upon Sherman's Creek. The 'Meadows in the Bay of Hellgate' were reserved to the church, to be used or rented for its benefit, with the bouwland in the Village set apart for the same purpose."

Riker's Hist. of Harlem, p. 192.

At any rate, if these particular meadows had not been allotted to the church before the advent of the British, they passed to the Town of New Harlem under the Nicolls patent and the allotment was made by the Town authorities.

It appears by the Town records under date of June 14th, 1667, that, " John Montagne, Jr., was permitted to have, in case of exchange, the church lots, meadows lying in the *bend of Hellgate*; provided he leave instead a piece of meadow, lying south of the Great Meadow, belong to number 1." The Great Meadow, was that upon the North side of Sherman's Creek, No. 1, referred to the lot on Jochem Peters' Flat, which Montagne gave up to the *Town in* 1661.

Montagne then secured from the Tappan Indians the following bill of sale :

"On this 29th August 1669, old style, the under written Indians have sold to me, John La Montagne, the Point named Rechewanis, bounded between two creeks and hills and behind a stream which runs to Montagne's Flat; *with the Meadows from the bend of Hellgate* to **Komande Kong.**"

Sellers of the Point	Rechewackan, Achwaarœwes, Sacharoch, Pasachkeegine, Niepenonhan, Konhamwon, Kottaron.	Tappan.

Montagne subsequently and on 8th February, 1672, obtained the deed of confirmation for the Point and *Meadows in the* Bay of Hellgate, from the Town, as stated above under the head of Tidal Creeks.

See this deed appendix, B. 2.

Prior to obtaining the above mentioned deed from the authorities of the town, it appears from the Harlem records, dated May 18th, 1671, that John de La Montagne made an agreement to sell to John Louwe Bogert (otherwise Von

Schoonerwoert) "a piece of land named in the Dutch language, Montagne's Point, but by the Indians Rechewanis," with the meadows thereto attached, and the meadows lying in the Bay of Hellgate, "for 3,000 guilders in sewant, *i. e.*, wampum, or in grain at the price of sewant," 1,500 guilders to be paid May 1st, 1672, and the remaining 1,500 guilders one year afterwards. Possession to be given when the first payment was made.

See this agreement in full Appendix B, No. 1.

This first payment was duly made and Bogert went into possession of the farm in 1672 under the agreement. He came from Bedford, Long Island. Before the second payment became due Montagne died, and his widow Maria, who was sometimes called by her maiden name Vermilje, received the balance of the purchase money, and gave Bogert a deed for the place. It is probable that Montagne had devised the property to her, but of this there appears to be no record. The deed was given under the direction of the Magistrates of the Town as follows:

"Appeared before me Hendrick Vandervin, Secretary of the Town of New Harlem, and the afore-named witnesses, Mrs. Maria Vermilje, the widow of Jan de La Montagne, late Secretary of the Town, who had in his lifetime sold to Jan Louwe Van Schoonderwort, his piece of land called Montagne's Point, together with the meadows thereunto belonging, as shown by an abstract of the sale thereof, dated 18th May, 1671, and by indenture bearing date 8th February, 1672, for the sum of 3,000 guilders, of which sum the appearer, characterized as above, hereby acknowledges the receipt in full to the last penny, in the first place giving thanks to the buyer for his punctuality, and releasing him from all further demands. Therefore it has been ceded and conveyed, so the grantor hereby cedes and conveys the said piece of land, *and meadows thereunto belonging* to him, the buyer in free and true possession, as they were possessed by her, without that she the appearer, or her heirs thereto shall claim any right. . . . .

"Thus done and executed at New Harlem on the 30th day of the month of March, 1674.
"MARIA MONTAGNE.
"Witnesses:
"DAVID DES MARET,
"DANIEL TOURNEUR."

On the 16th day of January, 1673, the constables and magistrates passed a resolution fixing the amount of Bogert's land at sixteen morgen. This estimate did not include the meadows. They did not form the basis for claims to allotments of the common lands.

See Appendix, B 9.

Although the deed from the town to Montagne, and from the Montagnes to Bogert, embraced all the meadows in the Bay of Hellgate, Joost Von Oblinus, who owned a farm on the Northerly part of Hoorn's Hook, adjoining Montagne's on the South, claimed a small section of the meadows in the Southern extremity of the Bay. He procured a citation for Bogert to appear at the next Court day and answer "why he has forbidden him to set off his meadows" (*i. e.* fence them in). The case came on trial in December, 1677, of which we have the following account.

"Whereas a dispute has arisen between Joost Von Oblinus and Jan Louwe Van Schonewert over a certain small meadow *lying in the Bay of Hellgate*, which each of the parties claims as belonging to him; after several rebates and rebuts on either side, it was decided by the Honorable Court, the said small meadow, being the most Southerly of the range under against the steep hill, next the kill, that John Louwe (Bogert) for his meadows shall have those that stretch from the great kill from Ancher's house; the rest to Joost Von Oblinus. And ordered that each shall bear his own costs attaching to this."

See Appendix B, No. 5.
Also Ricker, *supra*, p. 406.

This case shows that these meadows were worth going to law about at that early day, and serves to identify them. The presumption is that the decision of the Court was based upon evidence of the possession and title of the respective parties. The division line established by this judgment continued to be the permanent boundary line between the two farms.

The creek which formed the division line began at 96th Street and First Avenue, and ran about west, crossing the Second Avenue at 95th Street, and terminated at the steep rocky hill at about 94th Street between Second and Third Avenues. Von Oblinus subsequently sold his farm to John De Lamater.

> See Holmes Map of the Margaret McGown Estate which exhibits this creek and boundary line.
> Also Map, Appendix I.
> Also Appendix B, 3.
> Resolution of the Magistrates, &c., fixing Bogert lands at 18 morgen.

In 1691, the Patentees and Freeholders of Harlem determined to divide a part of the unappropriated or common lands, and caused them to be surveyed and laid out into lots and parcels, whereof each inhabitant of the town was to draw a part, every one according to his estate or property then possessed in severalty. Adolph Meyer, Jan Hendriese Brevoort, Samuel Waldron and Peter Van Oblinus were appointed to make these allotments, and transfer the titles with the aid of Adrion Appel, surveyor.

The parcel or lot No. 25 fell to John L. Bogert by virtue of his ownership of Montagne's Point Farm. The deed of the town is dated March 21st, 1701, and the lot is described as follows: "There is set off for John Louwe Bogert, for the right of sixteen *morgen*, and an *erf* right; a piece of land lying in *the bend of Hellgate;* beginning at the Southwest corner of the Hop Garden by a birch tree, till to a white oak tree, which stands by a small swamp (creupelbosje) marked J. L. B. and J. D. L., thence toward the river, past a rock marked J. L. B. and J. D. L., and *so on the beach, till to the end of a meadow,* north of a rocky hill; *as it is at present fenced in.*"

See this deed, Appendix B., No. 6.

This lot 25 contained 14 *morgen, i. e.,* 28 acres. It will be noticed that the description carries *it to the end of the meadow and that the lot is fenced in.* This adjoined Bogert's farm on the south and so much of the meadow as lay east of the lot was no doubt included in the description by way of confirmation of Bogert's title. He had already purchased those meadows from Montagne, and it was in regard to the small parcel at the southern extremity that he had the suit with Von Oblinus above mentioned. As the property had been drawn by and alloted to him in 1691, it is probable he had already gone into possession before the deed was delivered. His controversy with Von Oblinus shows that the parties were very particular about fencing in their property. Bogert's wife was the owner of the Hop Garden mentioned in the deed.

See the deed to her from Maria Vermilje, widow of Montagne, Appendix B, No. 4.

By the allotment of 1691, lot No. 26 was set over to Jan De Lamater, who at that time owned eight of "The ten Lots" situate on Hoorn's Hook, and consisting of 68 acres and bounding said lot 25 on the south. The Town's deed to him is dated March 21st, 1701. Lot 26 is described as "A piece of land lying in the *Bay of Hellgate,* extending from the northwest corner of the end of his lots to a white oak tree marked J. D. L. and J. L. B. *and so onward by the strand to the end of the meadow,* north of a rocky hill.

See Appendix B, 7. Also map showing the lots, Appendix I.

Lot 26 contained ten *morgen;* it and 25 were composed principally of the high rocky ground bordering on and lying mainly to the west and south of the meadows which extended to the East or Harlem River, the remainder of the meadows being included in the land then owned by Bogert and known as the Montagne's Point farm and meadows.

Lot 26 was subsequently included in the well-known farm of Samuel Waldron. Resolved Waldron never owned this farm, as some suppose; Samuel Waldron bought it in 1710 from the heirs of Jan De Lamater. In the deed to him it is described as follows: "All that tract of land commonly called or known as Hoorn's Hook, aforesaid, with all and singular the houses, house lots, lots of land, now in the possession of the said Samuel Waldron, as they are hereinafter named, expressed, bounded and numbered, that is to say: on the south, over against Hog Island, alais Forcans Island, by the river of Harlem; on the southwest by lot number 2, now in the possession of Margaret Codrington, widow; on the northwest by the patent line of Harlem; on the north by a white oak stump upon the bounds of the lands now in the possession of Barent Waldron and John Benson; on the northeast by a rock marked on the northeast side thereof L. B., on the southwest by L. M., *and so goes down to the said river* by several marked trees with the aforesaid letters, and runs on the north side of a rocky hill, and on the south side *by a piece of meadow and thence along the river* to said lot number 2; including all points, *meadows and marshes*, within the bounds above mentioned; containing by estimation one hundred and fifteen acres, be the same more or less."

The farm remained intact during the life of Samuel Waldron. His son William came into possession of it in 1741. He set off lots 3 and 4 to his brother Benjamin, and on Nov. 29th sold 21¼ acres at the southerly side of the farm to Jacob Leroy, which subsequently became the country seat of Com. Chauncey, but otherwise the farm underwent no material change, until it was divided by the heirs of William Waldron. The country seats of Astor, Gracia, Prime and Rhinelander were included in this farm.

Riker's Hist. p. 597.

The title to the Bogert farm passed to Johannes Benson by the following deed:

	DEED.
John Lowesen Bogert and Cornelia his wife, to Johannes Benson.	Dated Sept. 21, 1706. Ackd. Feby. 10th, 1707. Recd. Sept. 21, 1827. Liber 226 of Convs., p. 37. Cons. £650.

It will be noticed that this deed was not recorded until one hundred and twenty-one years after its date. The recitals in this deed are so interesting and important that they are set forth in full for convenience of reference.

"Whereas, John De La Montagne, late of Harlem, aforesaid yeoman, deceased, by instrument of sale bearing date the 18th day of May, Anno Dom. 1671, for the consideration therein mentioned did bargain and sell unto the said John Lowesen Bogert a certain parcel of land and meadows, commonly called Montagne's Point, and by the Indians or natives of the country called Recowanis, the said land and meadows being bounded on the north side with a kill or creek commonly called Montagne's kill, stretching from the East River to a certain fresh run or kill running betwixt Montagne's Plains and the aforesaid point, bounded on the south with a run and kill and a meadow, with hills till it meets with the aforesaid fresh run or kill over which runs the King's Highway, *together with the meadows lying in the Bay of Hellgate*, which the said Montagne had in exchange for a Town's lot of meadow:

"And whereas it so pleased God that the said John De La Montagne came to die, before all the conditions in the said bill of sale were duly to be performed; And whereas afterwards the said John Lowesen Bogert paid the remainder of the consideration money in the said Indenture of sale mentioned to Maria, the widow and relict of said John De La Montagne, and the said Maria, by a certain deed or instrument in writing bearing date the 30th day of March, Anno Dom. 1674, did confirm, transport and make over to him, the said John Lowesen Bogert, all the above described premises, as by the said instrument, relation being thereto had more fully and at large may appear.

"And whereas the said Maria, widow of said John De La Montagne, by her certain bill of sale bearing date the 4th day of November, Anno Dom. 1679, for the considerations therein mentioned, did grant, bargain and sell to the said Cornelia, the wife of the said John Lowesen Bogert, being authorized by her said husband to purchase a certain Hop Garden, lying at the rear of the land heretofore sold to the said John Lowesen Bogert by the said John De La Montagne and Maria his wife, betwixt the said land and the hill thereto adjoining, with all the right and title thereto belonging as by the said bill of sale, relation being thereto had to the same may at large appear; And whereas the patentees and freeholders of the town of Harlem aforesaid, at a town meeting held at the said town on the 11th day of December, Anno Dom. 1691, did make choice of Adolph Myer, Jan Hendricsen Brevoort, Samuel Waldron and Peter Van Oblinus to lay out the undivided lands, *belonging to the said town's patent* as by the minute or order thereof being entered in the public Register of the said town's affairs, signed by 16 of the said patentees, freeholders and inhabitants of said town at large may appear.

"And whereas the said patentees and freeholders, at another town meeting, held the 4th day of January, A. D. 1699, then unanimously consented and it was agreed and concluded, that each freeholder should be obliged to pay his proportion of all public charges that occurred in said town, proportionably to the land they had within the limits of the said town, and should likewise have a right to receive their just proportion of the undivided lands belonging to the said town, proportionable to their said quantity of lands by them held and enjoyed, as by the order or agreement entered likewise in the Public Register of said own and signed by 22 of the said patentees and freeholders, relation being had to the same at large, will appear; and whereas, the said John Lowesen Bogert, by virtue of the above-recited Instrument of sale stood then lawfully seized of the said parcel of land, called Montagne's Point and meadows thereto adjoining, which by computation contains 16 *morgen* or thereabout, be it more or less; and also the Hop Garden above mentioned:

"And whereas, the said John Lowesen Bogert, in compliance with the said order last above mentioned, hath ever since, from time to time, paid his share of the taxes and town charges, proportionable to the contents of the lands which he held and enjoyed, as by the tax rolls of book of town rates at large may appear:

"And whereas, said Adolph Myer, John Hendricsen Brevoort, Samuel Waldron and Peter Van Oblinus, pursuant to the trust in them reposed, and the authority to them given and granted to them as aforesaid, on the 21st of March, A. D. 1701, made their return to the Magistrates of the town, that among other parcels of land by them laid out, a lot for John Lowesen Bogert for right of 16 *morgen* of land, and one lot of land then in his possession, viz.: All that certain parcel of land lying in the bought of Hellgate, beginning on the southwest corner of the Hop Garden, by a *broken boom* or birch tree, running to a white-oak tree which stands by a small swamp marked with the letters I. L. B. and the letters I. L. D., towards the river, running by a rock marked I. L. B. and I. D. L., and running towards the strand or riverside to the end of the meadow on the north of a stony hill, as it was then and is now known by the name of the lot No. 48 (this lot is really 25, and is erroneously called 48 in the deed) and which joins to the south side of the above-mentioned land and meadows of him, the said John Lowesen Bogert, as by the said return and the approbation of the overseers and Magistrates of Harlem aforesaid, on the same likewise entered in the Public Register of said town will appear, relation being to the same had, which said lot of land as above butted and bounded was likewise confirmed to the said

John Lowesen Bogert, his heirs and assigns forever, by conveyance from Joost Oblinus, the surviving patentee or joint tenant, in the old patent of Harlem, for the considerations therein mentioned as by the said conveyance bearing date —— day of February, A. D. 1701, at large will appear, relation being had to the same and. which was likewise by Adolph Myer, John Hendricsen Brevoort and Samuel Waldron, and Peter Van Oblinus . . . Indenture bearing date the 14th day of September, A. D. 1706, as trustees for the said town of Harlem, confirmed and re-leased to the said John Lowesen Bogert, as by the said Indenture relation being thereto had more fully and at large will appear.

"Now this Indenture witnesseth that the said John Lowesen Bogert and Cornelia his wife, for and in consideration of 1,650 current money of New York, to them well and truly in hand paid by the said Johannes Benson before the ensealing and delivery hereof, the receipt whereof they do hereby acknowledge, and themselves to be herewith fully satisfied, contented and paid, and thereof and therefrom every part and parcel thereof they do freely, fully and absolutely acquit, release, exonerate and discharge him, the said Johannes Benson, his heirs, executors, administrators and assigns, and by these presents have given, granted, bargained, sold, conveyed, enfeofft, assured, confirmed, and by these presents give, grant, bargain, sell, convey, enfeoff, assure, and confirm unto the said Johannes Benson, his heirs and assigns all and every, the above recited or mentioned *parcels of land and meadows*, as they are in the above recitals particularly expressed, butted, bounded and granted to him the said John Lowesen Bogert and Cornelia his wife, together with all and singular the buildings, erections, houses, barns, stables, out-houses, orchards, gardens, fences, meadows, *marshes, swamps, creek's, ponds, waters, water-courses, springs, fountains, privileges,* improvements, paches, passages, commons and common of pasture, wood, underwood, privileges in the undivided lands and appurtenances whatsoever to the same granted parcels of land and meadows of right belonging and appertaining, and the reversion and reversions, remainder and remainders, rents, issues and profits of the same, and all and every part and parcel thereof, as also all deeds, writings, touching and concerning the premises hereby granted, and all the estate, right, title, dower, interest, property, possession, claim and demand whatsoever of them, the said John Lowesen Bogert and Cornelia his wife, of, in and to the same, or all or any part or parcel thereof:

"To have and to hold all and singular the said parcel of lands, meadows, and premises, before in these presents granted and recited to him the said Johannes Benson, his heirs and assigns forever, yielding and rendering and paying yearly and every year, to the Queen's Majestic, her heirs and successors, or such as shall be authorized to receive the same, his proportion of the quit rent reserved in the General Patents of Harlem, according to the quantity of land hereby granted."

Johannes Benson died in 1718, leaving a last will and testament dated May 9, 1711, proved May 20, 1718, recorded Liber 9 of Wills, p. 1, whereby he gives his whole estate to his wife, Elizabeth, for life, with remainder to his children.

On March 28, 1721, his widow and children conveyed the same property to his son, Samson Benson. This deed does not appear to be recorded.

See Riker's History of Harlem, p. 485.

Without regard to this missing deed, strictly speaking, there is no break in the chain of title, Samson Benson being one of the devisees and heirs at law of Johannes. Samson Benson went into possession of the property, and that was the possession of all the tenants in common, so far as the preservation of the title was concerned, and was good against every one, except his co-tenants.

Washburn's Real Property, 5th Ed., Vol. I., p. 689.
Florence v. *Hopkins*, 46 N. Y., p. 186.

As against the co-tenants the title may also be assumed

to be good. The fact of the open and exclusive possession of Samson Benson for so many years prior to his death; the license of the Town of Harlem to him to build the milldam and run the mill; the subsequent exclusive possession of his widow and children, and their conveyance of the whole property to Benjamin Benson, the open and exclusive occupation of the property by him, and those claiming under him, for a period, to the present time of 170 years, amount to evidence of original ouster by Samson Benson and the disseizin of his co-tenants, in common.

Washburn's Real Property, Id., Vol. 1, p. 690-91.
Florence v. *Hopkins*, Id., p. 186.
Also, *Culver* v. *Rhodes*, 87 N. Y. 353.

Samson Benson died possessed of the said property. He left a last Will and Testament, dated September 12, 1739; it was proved January 21, 1741, and recorded the same day in the office of the Surrogate in Liber 14, of Wills, p. 157. By this Will he gives all his property, after the death or marriage of his wife Mary, to his children; with a provision, that his said dwelling house, farm and mills shall be sold within six weeks after the death or marriage of his said wife, to any one of his children who might desire to purchase the same.

Johannes Benson and Fanneken his wife, Adolph Benson and Eva his wife, Jacob Dickman, Jr., and Cateline his wife, all of Harlem, in the County of New York, and others,

To

Benjamin Benson, of Harlem, in the County of New York.

DEED.

Dated January 28, 1742.
Recorded July 19, 1808.
Liber 80 of Convs. p. 498.
Cons. £1,500.

Conveys the following described premises:

All that certain dwelling house, mills and farm as it is

now in fence, situate, lying and being in Harlem in the County and Province of New York, now in the tenor or occupation of him the said Benjamin Benson, containing about two hundred acres, be the same more or less. Also a lot, number eighteen in a third division containing five acres, three quarters and two roods, the same containing in breadth about nineteen rods and a half, and runs from the middle line in Division between the land of Mattje and Lawrence Cornelison and some common land South ; fifty-three degrees East to the meadows at Harlem River, also another lot, number eighteen, in the fourth division, containing five acres, three quarters and twenty-two rods, being in breadth eighteen rods, and runs from a North, North-west line, drawn from the [   ] of John Dickman's land sixty degrees West between Isaac Delamatre, and some common land to Hudson River, which premises were purchased by the said Samson Benson from Elizabeth Benson and others by a deed bearing date the 28th day of March, in the year of our Lord, One thousand, seven hundred and twenty-one, reference being thereunto had will more at large appear. Together with all and singular the buildings, erections, houses, barns, stables, out houses, orchard, gardens, fence, meadows, marshes, swamps, creeks, ponds, water, water courses, springs, streams, fountains, privileges, improvements, paths, passages, common and right of commage, woods, underwood, trees, timber, rights, liberties, profits, hereditaments and appurtenances, whatsoever to the said, hereby granted and released premises belong or in any wise appertaining.

Benjamin Benson,

To

Samson Benson.

DEED.

Dated May 2, 1791.
Acknowledged May 2, 1791.
Recorded August 31, 1791.
Liber 46, of Convs. p. 558.
Cons. 5 s., and natural love and affection.

Conveys a tract of land with buildings. Beginning at a black oak stump at the corner of land belonging unto Lawrence Benson, on the South side of Mill Creek or pond; running southwestly along said Lawrence Benson's land to a run of water, and along said run of water till it meets the Commons; thence southerly to land formerly belonging to Benjamin Waldron, deceased; then along said Benjamin Waldron's land to the land of William Waldron, deceased; thence easterly along said land to the drowned meadows or marsh; thence northerly and easterly along said meadows or marsh, till it comes to the mouth of the above mentioned mill creek; thence westerly along said mill creek or pond to the place of beginning, *including all the estate of the said Benjamin Benson and Susannah, his wife, to the southward of said Mill Creek or pond* and whereon the said Samson Benson now lives or resides.

It is immaterial whether this deed is construed to run along their outer or inner line of the meadows or marshes, because it conveys *all the estate* of the grantor and wife *to the southward of Mill Creek or pond*, and consequently includes the marshes or meadows. The title of the southerly farm extended to the centre of the creek east of the mill-dam. The grantor intended to convey all this farm. For further observations in relation to this deed see the abstract relating to Harlem Creek.

Chapter X, *post*.

Samson Benson, the above-named grantee, died intestate, January 31, 1821, in possession of the premises set forth in the last deed, leaving him surviving Margaret, the wife of Andrew McGown, his only child and heir-at-law. All the meadows between Hoorn's Hook and Montagne's Point, were subsequently known as the McGown Meadows or Marshes. They differed in no essential respect from the rest of the Harlem Meadows, as is shown by the above references in regard to the meadows, and the by maps compiled by Randall, Dripp, Viele and Colton's Topographical Map of 1836. Such Meadows are included under the legal definition of dry land.

Hall on Sea-shores, p. 7, *De Jure Maris*, Chapter VI, *supra*.

Even should it be conceded that these marshes were in some places, and to a considerable extent, somewhat below the level of the mean high tide, it would have no material bearing on the question as to the origin of the titles. These lands were sufficiently elevated to produce grasses, and a vegetation useful to the farmers for the purposes of husbandry, and highly prized by them. They clearly came within the broad and comprehensive terms of the patents, granting, " *All the soils, creeks, waters, meadows, pastures and marshes.*" These grants were by express terms included in the confirmation patent of Governor Dongan to the freeholders and inhabitants of Harlem, of March 7th, 1686.

The history of these meadows extend to a period of more than two hundred years, and to the time of the earliest settlements on that part of the Island. For all that period their ownership has been claimed by private persons. The title to them has come down undivided and unbroken until 1834, when Mrs. Margaret McGown, conveyed part of them to her son, Samson Benson McGown, by deed recorded in Liber 306, page 70. In 1835 she conveyed the remainder of the meadows to Edward Sanford, the eminent and gifted member of the New York Bar, who perished in the wreck of the United States Mail Steamship Arctic of the Collins Line, which went down in mid ocean in 1855. The deeds to Mr. Sanford were recorded Feby. 4th, 1835, in Liber 320, pp. 484 and 486 of conveyances. These conveyances included all the meadows in the bay except the range originally belonging to Von Oblinus and which afterwards came to be possessed by Abraham Duryea.

No doubt seems to have been entertained as to the nature of these meadows, or that they were included in the grants to the Town of Harlem, until after the opening and construction of the avenues and intersecting streets across them, by reason of which the meadows were destroyed and disappeared, and gave place to unsightly mud flats. Then some members of the Bar, doubtless ignorant of their early history and appearance, began to entertain the opinion that these lands may have been, and probably were, within the limits of the tideway, and consequently that the title to them was in the City of New York, by virtue of the Charter made by Governor Dongan on April 22d, 1686, granting to the City "all the waste vacant, unpatented and unappropriated lands in said City and on Manhattan Island extending to low water mark and not heretofore granted by any former Governor."

This charter was a month and a half subsequent to the confirmation patent of Governor Dongan to the freeholders and inhabitants of Harlem. The grant to the City of New York, is only of the *unappropriated and unpatented* lands. It was expressly limited to lands "*not heretofore granted* by any former Governor." The Charter did not disturb the rights already acquired under the Harlem patents or in any other way.

There are two answers to this objection: The first is that, by the common law, the salt marshes are not part of the seashore or strand or of the waste lands. They are *prima facie* not part of the vacant lands, because such lands, by the same law belong to the subject and even the king can not obtain title to them, except by prescription, grant, forfeiture, escheat, &c.

Bristow v. *Cormican*, (3 App. Cas. 641, *supra*.)

So that without regard to the previous Harlem patents, or the reservation of previous grants in the Dongan Charter by legal presumption, these lands would not pass under that charter; because, as a matter of fact, the Harlem marshes were in actual possession of the freeholders and inhabitants of Harlem before the advent of Governor Nicholls, and that he recognized their claims to the whole territory of Harlem and the marshes generally. This appears from the language of the patent, namely, " Whereas there *is* a certain Town or Village commonly called or known by the name of New Harlem . . . now in the *tenure* or *occupation* of several freeholders and inhabitants." The words *tenure* or *occupation*, are a strong phrase, under the circumstances. This being a country held by discovery and Harlem being but recently settled, title by occupancy, might with propriety imply a grant.

Governor Nicholl's decision in respect to John Archer's intrusion upon some of the marshes in the Harlem River (*supra*) acknowledges the pre-existing title of the inhabitants of Harlem to the marsh lands.

De Jure Maris, Ch. 6, *supra*, and
Hall's Seashores, p. 10, *supra*.

The second answer is as above stated, namely, the marshes had been already granted by the Harlem patents.

In considering this question, of the supposed claim under the Dongan Charter, it should not be forgotten that the Corporation of New York has always been very jealous in respect to its territorial rights, and especially so in regard to its claim to the land between high and low water and its jurisdiction along the shore front of the entire Island, nor that it has generally had the benefit of the advice and guidance in legal questions of experienced and learned lawyers, while in matters relating to hydrography and topography it has had the service of able and experienced engineers and surveyors.

It is altogether improbable that a claim to so large and important a piece of shore front should have remained unknown and unenforced by the City officials for so many generations. The City has never asserted any claim to these marshes, nor to the intersecting creeks, but on the contrary it has by its acts in relation to street improvements, taxation, and the water front of the City, shown that it does not own, or claim to own the ground. In fact it has, in effect, through its duly constituted legal advisers, expressly disclaimed having any title or claim of title, not only to the McGown marshes, but also to any portion of the original common lands of Manhattan Island, northerly of the division line between the City of New York and the town of Harlem, as established by the acts of the Colonial Assembly and Council of 1772, 1774 and 1775.

Vide, the opinion of the Hon. Richard O'Gorman, as

Counsel to the Corporation of the City of New York, furnished to the Comptroller under date of August 1st, 1870, and the opinion of the Hon. William C. Whitney, likewise furnished as Corporation Counsel, to the Comptroller, under date of November 10th, 1880. These opinions are on file in the office of the Law Department of the City. Authentic copies are given in the Appendix under the letters D and E.

CONCLUSION.

From the deeds, Harlem Patents, and historic and other evidence available, and a due consideration of the law applicable to such lands, it ought to be apparent to every unprejudiced mind, that the doubts in regard to the titles to these meadows, with the intersecting creeks, are wholly groundless, and they could have been dispelled before taking shape by an impartial and proper investigation of the subject.

The meadows or marshes in the bay between Hoorn's Hook and Montagne's Point were a distinct formation of land at the time of the first settlements of Harlem. Their extent and outlines were then substantially the same as when the greater part of them came to be possessed by Margaret McGown in 1821. The title, as derived through the Montagnes, John Louwe Bogert, Joost Von Oblinus and John De La Mater and the Town of Harlem, appears to be good and valid. It is one of the most ancient, and best authenticated titles on the Manhattan Island.

CHAPTER X.

The Harlem Creek, the Harlem Mill Pond, and Van Keulen's Hook.

PART FIRST.

Of all the numerous creeks which penetrated the Island of Manhattan, one of the largest, most important, and most interesting, was the kill Rechawanes, subsequently known in the annals of Harlem as Montagne's Kill, Benson's Creek, and Harlem Creek. It divided the farms of the two first landed proprietors and settlers at Harlem, Hendrick De Forest and Jacob Van Curler, the close friend of Director Wouter Van Twiller. The kill was the outlet of three fresh-water streams. The principal one had its rise at Claremont near the Hudson and not far from the spot now occupied by the tomb of General Grant. The second rose in the high hills west of the Ninth Avenue, near 108th Street, and the third issued from a spring called "The Fountain," in the elevated ground now enclosed in the northerly part of Central Park. The last stream formed the division line between Montagne's Flat and Montagne's Point.

The spring is still flowing and may be seen not far from the place where McGown's Pass led down to Harlem Plains, in the bridle-path of Central Park, near the junction of the former lines of Sixth Avenue and 104th Street. It supplies the water for a drinking fountain at which equestrians may water their horses. The creek attained its importance from the fact that the Harlem Mill was built near its margin, and it supplied the power to run the mill.

The following historical facts are compiled mainly from Riker's History of Harlem.

The project of erecting a mill upon this creek was under discussion in 1661, at the time the Montagne family petitioned the Director and Council for permission to establish a settlement upon their deserted farm Vredendal. The work was deferred until after the occupation of the English. Governor Nicolls was accompanied in his expedition by Thomas Delavall, a captain in the British army, and one of Nicolls' suite. He was made Treasurer of the Colony, and subsequently Mayor of New York, and was the first person named in the second Nicolls patent of 1667. He became one of the largest landed proprietors in Harlem. In January, 1667, he made a proposal to build the mill if the inhabitants of the town would construct the dam. He requested leave to erect a stone house on the land adjoining his land (on Van Keulen's Hook) near the mill, and to fortify it for a place of refuge for the villagers in time of need. He also desired permission to run a fence straight from the fence now standing to the stone bridge upon Van Keulen's Hook, and to use the land and meadows so enclosed. The inhabitants agreed to make the dam for the mill, provided they might enjoy the benefits according to custom. They also agreed to the erection of the house near the mill and the setting off the land and meadows mentioned in the request. After much labor the mill-dam was finished during 1667. It crossed the creek just west of the present Third Avenue. Near its northern end Delavall built the mill.

See Appendix B, No. 8.

The land which Delavall took for mill purposes adjoined his land. It belonged to the town, and formed the northern boundary of the mill-pond. It was afterwards known as the Mill Camp.

The mill is next mentioned in the Harlem records under the date of June 8, 1669. The mill-dam lately "impaired by breach of water" needed prompt attention. Captain Delavall was then abroad, and Governor Lovelace, being informed of the accident, ordered " John Askew and Peter Van Nest, of Flatlands, to go to Harlem forthwith, with their workmen, and use their best skill and endeavour in repairing the dam, and whatever else is required about the Mill."

On August 8, 1676, Captain Delavall conveyed to his son-in-law, James Carteret and Frances his wife, "All that messuage, tenement and farm" which he (Delavall) formerly bought of one Moseman, "situate, lying, and being in the town of Harlem, within or upon a certain island called or known by the name of Manhattan Island; *and all that water mill* which the said Thomas Delavall built or caused to be built, situate, lying, and being in and upon Manhattan Island aforesaid, together with all the lands and meadows and pastures to the said mill belonging or adjoining, or therewithal usually held, used, occupied and enjoyed."

The lot bought by Delavall of Moseman, referred to in this deed, was No. 22 on Van Keulen's Hook.

See Map, Appendix I.

Van Keulen's Hook was laid out by the authorities of the town in 1661, and divided into 22 lots of equal breadth, all running from the river or creek to the northerly line, and designed to contain three *morgen* (*i. e.*, six acres) each. As the lines were of unequal length, the contents were unequal. To remedy this a new survey was made in 1676, by which some of the lots were lessened in width, and the contents equalized.

See Map annexed to Riker's Hist. of Harlem.

No. 1 was the most easterly lot, and No. 22 the most westerly. Lot 22 was originally allotted to John Le Roy, who sold it to Moseman, who conveyed it to Delavall.

See Mr. James Riker's statement, Appendix B, 10.

The town subsequently set off another lot from the town lands adjoining 22 on the west, and conveyed it to Delavall as No. 23. This was done to take the place of No. 21, which Delavall claimed. These two lots, 22 and 23, embracing about 12 acres, were included in the above deed by Delavall to Carteret and wife. They adjoined the Mill Camp on the east. Delavall built the mill on lot 22.

Captain James Carteret and his wife Frances died prior

to August 11, 1705. They left a son, George, who died without issue, and a daughter, Elizabeth, who was married in the Island of Jersey, November 11, 1699, to Philip Pipon of Noiremont. On August 11, 1705, Pipon and wife, then residing in London, empowered Thomas Newton, of Boston, N. E., to enter upon and take "legal possession of all their lands upon Manhattan Island and Little Barnes Island, or elsewhere in America, whereof she, Elizabeth (or he, Pipon in her right) is seized, interested, or entitled as granddaughter, or heir of Thomas Delavall, deceased, or as daughter or heir of her father or mother, James Carteret, Esq., and Frances W. his wife, or either of them, or as survivor or heir of George Carteret, Esq.; also authorizing said Newton to lease said premises for a term not exceeding five years."

What Newton did, if anything, is not known. Mrs. Pipon died in Jersey in November, 1720, leaving her surviving, her husband Philip, and two sons, James and Elias. The father, Philip, subsequently entailed upon his son James and his heirs male his estate in Jersey, and upon his son Elias and his heirs male, his property in America. Elias, being 24 years of age, came to New York to look after his possessions. He built upon Little Barent's Island, which he re-named Belle Isle, and married Blanche, daughter of John Lafons. His property being mainly unproductive, he petitioned the Colonial Assembly to remove the entail and empower him to sell a part of his land in order that he might improve the rest.

Notice of his intentions were publicly read in the church at Harlem, by the parish clerk, on the three succeeding Sundays, beginning September 27, 1730, and duly certified by the Governor and Council, October 15 following. The Application was not acted upon during that session of the Assembly, nor does it appear what became of it. By releases executed in the Island of Jersey May 18, 19, 1732, James released to Elias all his interest in the lands in Harlem, and Elias released to James all his interest in the lands in Jersey.

Elias Pipon, having become insolvent about the latter part of 1735, executed a deed in trust for the benefit of his creditors to Simon Johnson, John Auboyneau and James Faviere, his wife joining in it.

Pipon and two of the assignees, Auboyneau and Faviere, having died, the execution of the trust devolved on the survivor, Simon Johnson, who conveyed the two lots, 22 and 23 on Van Keulen's Hook, to Benjamin Benson, as follows.

Simon Johnson	Warrantee Deed.
To	Dated Sept. 25th, 1747.
Benjamin Benson.	Consideration £171, current money.

Conveys, "All that piece of land, situate lying and being within the Township of New Harlem, in the out ward of the City of New York, aforesaid, upon Van Keulen's Hook, known or called by the name of Delavall's Land contiguous or adjourning westerly to a certain parcel of land, commonly called the Mill Camp, easterly to the land of Dirck Benson, southerly to Harlem Mill Creek, and northerly to the road or highway, if it does so far extend, containing six *morgen*, be it more or less, together with all and singular the *fences*, *meadows*, lands, waters, water courses, profits, emoluments, advantages, easements, ways, passages, hereditaments and appurtenances, etc." This description carried the title to the center of this creek, and included probably two-fifths of the space between the dam and First Avenue. This deed was put in evidence by the plaintiff in *Roberts* v. *Baumgarten et al* (51 *N. Y. Superior Court*).

See printed case on appeal.

Owing to the disuse of the mill by Delavall and his family, the privilege of using the Mill Camp for mill purposes lapsed. This led to a grant being made by the town on October 23d, 1738, to Samson Benson, of similar privileges to those granted to Delavall in 1667. Samson Benson was the oldest son of Johannes Benson, who purchased

Montagne's Point farm from Bogert, and was now the owner of that farm.

He was authorized to place the mill on the Mill Camp, with a dam wherever it might suit him best. He built the mill on his farm on the southerly side of the stream, and had scarcely finished it in 1740 when he died. His son Benjamin having purchased the farm from the widow and children succeeded to the mill right. Being owner of lots 22 and 23 Van Keulen's Hook, he made an application to the Town for the purchase of the Mill Camp, the same was awarded to him and the price was fixed by Lewis Morris, Abraham Van Wyck and Abraham Lefferts, Arbitrators, appointed by the town. The consideration money was £160 current money. The award was made May 30th, 1758, by this description:

" Beginning at the fence of the said Benjamin Benson, by the Mill Creek and runs along his fence northwardly to Harlem road, about thirty one chains, thence along said road twenty three chains and one half, which is three chains beyond a large oak tree near Van Breemen's house, thence south, ten degrees east to said Mill Creek, thence along said creek to the place where it began."

See the instrument in full. Appendix B. 12

The description "by the Mill Creek" and " to the said Mill Creek, thence along said creek," carries the grant to the centre of the creek.

See the law as to Tidal Creeks, *ante*.

The northerly half of that part of the creek was owned by the Town of Harlem by virtue of the patents. The title to the southerly half of the Mill Pond was then owned by Benjamin Benson, his title being derived through the deed of the Town of Harlem to John Montagne the younger; and of the Director and Council of New Netherland to John Montagne, the elder, dated May 9th, 1647, conveying Montagne's Point. It is covered by the following description:

" A piece of land situate on the Island of Manhattans,

. . . lying betwixt two hills and a kill, *and a point named Recehwanes, stretching betwixt two kills.*" This is equivalent to saying, bounded by two kills, and carries the title to the centre of the streams.

See this deed, Appendix B, 2.
Also Map Appendix I.

This deed conveys the land on both sides of the Southerly creek, which divides the meadows attached to Montagne's Point, and the meadows in the Bay of Hellgate, and consequently includes all of the creek. The words "bounded on the Northerly side by a creek" carry it to the centre.

Thus Benjamin Benson became seized in fee simple to the title to the whole of the bed of the Mill Pond, and to the southerly half of the Mill Creek, easterly of the Mill dam, and to as much of the northerly half of that creek as lay opposite to the lots conveyed to him by Simon Johnson, assuming that Johnson owned that part of the creek.

See cases, *supra* and *post.*

During the Revolutionary War, the old mill on the southerly side of the creek was burnt. After the war Benjamin Benson built a new mill on his farm on the northerly side of the creek and also a substantial stone dwelling. In 1827, when the Harlem Canal was begun, the mill, a three-story frame building was taken down, but the dwelling house remained until 1865.

In 1748 Benjamin Benson acquired the title to 35 acres on Van Keulen's Hook from the estate of his grandfather, Adolph Myer, and on December 30th, 1755, and May 11th, 1764, he purchased two more lots on that tract from John Benson, son of Dirck Benson. The land lay together, adjoining his lots 22 and 23, and was bounded on the east by the farm of Peter Bussing. The property thus acquired on Van Keulen's Hook extended from the dam to First Avenue on the northerly side of Mill Creek, and with the Mill Camp constituted the greater part, if not the whole of Benson's farm on the north side of the creek.

Riker's Hist. 258, 262, 489, 591 and 600.

Benjamin Benson conveyed this property to his son Peter B., as follows:

Benjamin Benson To Peter B. Benson.	DEED. Dated Apl. 2, 1791. Recd. May 12, 1797. Liber 54 Conv. p. 321. Cons. 5 shillings.

"All that certain messuage or tenement, *being all my estate to the North of the Mill Pond between the fence of the widow Storm, and the Road leading to Harlem*, including the *Mill Stream* and *Mill and Mill Pond* with all its privileges and appurtenances, and to shut the Mill dam at the south side of the said Mill Pond where it now lays; and all and singular the houses, barns, buildings, water, water courses &c."

This deed and the one made by Benjamin Benson to his son Samson, of the farm on the southerly side of Harlem or Mill Creek, should be considered together, and with the surrounding circumstances, in order to arrive at a correct conclusion as to the intention of the grantor. Preliminarily it will be assumed that the center of Mill Creek and of Mill Pond originally formed the boundary line between the two farms; that subsequently the grantor included the whole of the Mill Pond in the northerly farm, and that at the time of these conveyances the farms were divided by the center of Mill Creek up to the dam, and by the southerly side of the Mill Pond west of the dam.

The deed made by Benjamin Benson to his son Samson, dated May 2, 1791, conveys the southerly farm. It was also a gift to his son. Although it bears date one month later than the deed to Peter, it was acknowledged on the day of its date and recorded August 31, 1791, whereas the deed to Peter was not acknowledged until May 10th, or eight days after, and was not recorded until May 12th, 1797, or more than five years after the deed to Samson, who was already in possession of the farm before receiving his deed. Presumably the deed to Samson was delivered first. But it is evident that the father's acts were intended to be concurrent, and the sons to be treated impartially.

Peter was to have the northerly farm, with all its improvements and appurtenances, and the whole of the Mill Pond, and Samson was to have the southerly farm and all that appertained to it.

The language in the deed to Peter, conveying "all that certain messuage or tenement *being all my estate to the northward of the mill pond*," shows that he intended to convey the entire farm on which he lived, and if that included the northerly half of the Mill Creek opposite, the title to it passed under the deed. In like manner the words at the end of the description in the deed to Samson Benson ("including all the estate of the said Benjamin Benson and Susannah, his wife, to the southward of said Mill Creek or pond"), would include the entire property southward of the center of the creek or division line between the two farms.

The description in the deed to Samson Benson is as follows:

"All that certain *tract or farm*, piece or parcel of land lying and being in the said town of Harlem and bounded as follows, viz.: Beginning at an oak stump at the corner of land belonging unto Lawrence Benson, on the South side of Mill creek or pond, running southwesterly along said Lawrence Benson's land to a run of water, and along said run of water, till it meets the commons; thence southerly to land formerly belonging to Benjamin Waldron, deceased, thence along said Benjamin Waldron's land to the land of William Waldron, deceased; thence easterly along said land to the drowned meadows or marsh, thence northerly and easterly along said meadows or marshes till it comes to the mouth of the above mentioned Mill Creek; thence westerly along said Mill Creek or pond to the place of beginning, *including all the estate of the said Benjamin Benson and Susannah his wife to the southward of said Mill Creek or pond and whereon the said Samson Benson now lives or resides.*"

This description, by metes and bounds, gives no measurements or specific distances. The starting point is on the bank of the creek, which also is the mill pond. The last two courses are *to the mouth of the creek and westerly along the creek or pond to the place of beginning.* This carries the title to the center of the creek and pond.

In *Luce* v. *Carley*, 24 Wendell, p. 453, Cowen, Judge, says: "It is never thought that monuments mentioned in such a deed as occupying the bank of a river are meant by the parties to stand on the precise water line at its high or low mark. They are used rather to fix the *termini* of the line which is described as following the sinuosities of the stream, leaving the law to say, as the line happens to be above or below tide water, whether the one half of the river shall be included, with the islands which lie on the side of the channel nearest to the line described. Where the grant is so framed as to touch the water of the river and the parties do not expressly except the river, if it be above tide, one-half of the bed of the stream is included by construction of law. If the parties meant to exclude it, they should do so by express exception.

"In the *Seneca Nation, etc.*, v. *Knight*, 25 N. Y. 498, the boundary was described as beginning at a post on the north bank of the Cattaraugus Creek, and thence ran, by various courses and distances, to a post on the north bank of the creek, thence down the same, and along the several meanders thereof, to the place of beginning, and it was held that the grant included the bed of the stream to the center. The Court approved the remark of Chancellor Walworth, in *Child* v. *Starr*, that monuments in such cases are only referred to as giving the directions of the lines to the river, or stream, and not as restricting the boundary on the river. The Court also remarked that in case of boundary on the river, monuments are never located in fact or in description, in the channel of a river, and that monuments were necessary in order to mark the places of intersection with the stream.

The language of Chancellor Walworth in *Child* v. *Starr*, 4 Hill, pp. 373, 375, is, "Running to a monument standing on the bank, and from thence running *by the river or along the river*, does not restrict the grant to the bank of the stream; for the monuments in such cases are only referred to as giving the directions of the line to the river, and not as restricting the boundaries on the river."

> See also opinion, Bradish, President, in the case of *Child* v. *Starr*, and the authorities under the head of Tidal Creeks.
> See also opinion of Redfield, J., in *Buck* v. *Squires* (22 Vt. 484, 494), which is a most able and comprehensive statement of the law of boundaries.
> See also *Rogers* v. *Jones* (1 Wend. 238), which shows that a grant on salt water is not limited to the high water line.

If the deed to Samson Benson be interpreted by itself it will include the southerly half of the Mill Creek and the southerly half of the Mill Pond; but taking the deed in connection with the concurrent deed to Peter B. Benson, and the evident intention of the grantor, the southerly half of the Mill Pond would be excluded, as the whole of the pond was expressly granted to Peter in his deed. The boundary line between the two farms would then be the center of the Mill Creek and the southerly line of the Mill Pond. The intention of the grantor was to dispose of the two farms in their entirety and reserve no right in the Mill Creek.

> See criticism of this deed, in Chap. IX, *ante*.
> Also Washburn's Real Property, 5th Ed. Vol. 3, pp. 421 to 438.

This interpretation of the deeds of Benjamin Benson to his sons, Samson and Peter B., was not brought to the attention of the Court either on the trial or on the appeals, in *Robert* v. *Baumgarten*, *supra*. The opinion of Sedgwick, Ch. J., and that of Gray, J., both hold that under the deed from Benjamin Benson to Peter B. Benson, his son, no title was acquired to any part of the Mill Creek east of the milldam. These opinions were put upon the twofold ground:

First, that the description in the deed did not include the property in controversy; and second, that part of the land claimed, being below high water mark in the creek, the presumption was that the title was in the people or the State representing them. But, as has been remarked above, under the subject of Tidal Creeks, the question of the title to Harlem Mill Creek was not before the Court, nor was the subject of the title of Benjamin Benson's title to it; neither was there any presentation of the law relating to small tidal streams. If that case had been fully and properly stated and discussed, it is not unreasonable to assume that the language of those decisions would have been quite different. The result of that controversy would have been the same, because the title of Peter B. Benson, under the most favorable construction of his deed, did not include any part of the bed of Mill Creek south of the centre line of it. But the decisions would not, by an erroneous application or the supposed common law, have cast doubts upon the title not only of Harlem Mill Creek, but also upon the titles to all small tidal streams, and upon the lands formerly occupied by such streams, where they have been filled in and obliterated. It is to be hoped that an opportunity may be presented to the Court of Appeals, at an early day, to examine the law relating to small tidal streams not navigable "for any useful purpose connected with trade, travel, or commerce;" and that the subject may be so fully and properly presented that the question may be finally determined and set at rest.

Peter (B.) Benson died in 1802, leaving a last will and testament dated June 27, 1801, proved before the Surrogate of the City and County of New York, January 3, 1803, and recorded in Liber 44 of Wills, p. 239, whereby he gives and devises unto his son Benjamin P. Benson, his heirs and assigns, "all that my land on which I now live (excepting eight acres) situate, lying and being in the township of Harlem, on the south side of the highway, extending to the East River, together with the mill and stream now leased to Samuel Denny, with all the building and improvements whatsoever. I also give and devise to my said son one-half of the wood-land and one-half of the salt meadows lying on the north side of the Post Road, to hold to him the said Benjamin P. Benson, his heirs and assigns forever.

"Item. I give and devise unto my daughter Wilhelmina Benson, her heirs and assigns, all the tillable land on the north side of the Post Road, together with the other half of the wood-land and salt meadow, with all the buildings and improvements, as also eight acres on the south side of the Bridge Road." Wilhelmina Benson afterwards married Peter Van Arsdale.

Benjamin P. Benson, Peter Van Arsdale and Wilhelmina his wife, made partition of the property devised to them by Peter B. Benson, as follows:

Benjamin P. Benson, son of Peter Benson, deceased, of the first part,

and

Peter Van Arsdale and Wilhelmina his wife, daughter of said Peter Benson, deceased, of the second part.

PARTITION DEED.

Dated Apl. 22d, 1818.
Ackd. do.
Recd. do.
Liber 127 of Conv. p. 302.

Conveys to parties of the second part: "All that certain piece or parcel of ground situate, lying and being in the town of Harlem between the Old Harlem Road and the Harlem Bridge Road, and beginning at the north side of the Bridge Road at the westerly line of the property belonging to Luke Kip, and running thence along the said road south 46°, west 28 chains, 23 links: thence north 6° 30', east 7 chains and 1½ links; thence south 63°, west 18 chains, 10 links; thence south 35° 45', east 2 chains; thence south 63°, west 4 chains and 30 links to Harlem Creek; thence along the creek as it runs and turns, to the Old Harlem Road; thence along the Old Harlem Road as it now runs, to the line of the land belonging to Luke Kip; thence along said Kip's line to the place of beginning, containing 27 acres. And also all that other piece or parcel of land situate between the Harlem Bridge Road and the Third Avenue, beginning at a point on the northwesterly side of the Third Avenue where the northeasterly line of 113th Street intersects said Avenue, running thence along the Avenue north 33° 30', east 5 chains 72 links to land of James Roosevelt; thence along the land of James Roosevelt 9°, west 9 chains 70 links to the Harlem Road; thence along the said road 46°, north 12 chains and 96 links to the middle fence; thence along the middle fence south 6° 45', east 27 links to the northeasterly side of 113th Street, and thence along the line of the said street south 56° 30', east 9 chains 13 links to place of beginning.

"The parties of the second part convey to the party of the first part : "All that certain piece or parcel of ground situate etc., at Harlem, lying on the southerly side of the Harlem Bridge Road, and extending thence to the East River, together with the Mill and stream. The said land is bounded on the east by land belonging to George Bradish, James Roosevelt, the heirs of Flamen Bull and John F. Jackson, being all the land of the said Peter Benson south of the said Harlem Bridge Road, except eight acres hereinbefore described and released by the said party of the first part, unto the said parties of the second part.

"And also all that piece of woodland and salt meadow lying on the north side of Harlem Bridge Road, beginning at the Harlem Creek, and running thence along the said road north 46°, east 16 chains and 14 links; thence north 6° and 31', east 7 chains 1½ links; thence south 35° and 45', east 2 chains; thence south 63°, west 4 chains and 30 links to Harlem Creek, thence along the creek as it winds and turns to the place of beginning."

Peter Van Arsdale and Wilhelmina his wife, To Benjamin L. Benson.	W. DEED, F. C. Dated July 6th, 1825. Recd. Nov. 3d, 1825. L. 193 of Conv. p., 480. Cons. $13,500.

Conveys some promises set off to the parties of the first part in the above mentioned partition deed.

Benjamin P. Benson and
Mary Ann his wife,

To

Benjamin L. Benson.

W. DEED, F. C.
Dated July 10th, 1825.
Ackd. Oct. 13th, 1825.
Recd. Nov. 3d, 1825.
L. 193 of Conv., p. 474.
Cons. $30,000.

Conveys the premises set apart to Benjamin P. Benson by the above mentioned partition deed.

Benjamin P. Benson and
Mary Ann, his wife,

To

Benjamin L. Benson.

DEED, B & S.
Dated July 10th, 1825.
Ackd. 16 March, 1826.
Recd. 25 March, 1826.
L. 200 of Conv., p. 546.
Cons. $10.00.

Conveys "All that certain piece of ground situate, lying and being in the twelfth ward of the City of New York, being part and parcel of the farm of Peter Benson, deceased, and known as the Harlem Bridge Road, extending from the Harlem Mill Pond or Creek to the northermost bounds of the farm of the said Peter Benson deceased.

Also the mill, the mill stream or pond attached to the mill; the ground, marsh or marshes covered by the said mill stream and the water courses and privileges, rights and appurtenances belonging thereto; also all the low lands, salt meadows, flats and marshes in front of and adjoining to the uplands which belonged to Peter Benson in his lifetime, situate along said creek."

Peter Van Arsdale and Wilhelmina, his wife,

To

Benjamin L. Benson.

DEED, B & S.
Dated July 6th, 1825.
Ackd. Sept. 12, 1825.
Recd. Nov. 3d, 1825.
Liber 193, Conv., p. 483.
Cons. $1.

Conveys, "All the low lands, meadows, marshes, flats covered with water, waters, water courses, lying adjacent to lands in Harlem formerly owned by Peter Benson of Harlem, deceased."

Benjamin L. Benson,

To

Harriet M. Wiswall.

DEED, B & S.
Dated Sept. 15, 1835.
Ackd. Oct. 12, 1835.
Rec. 17th Dec., 1835.
Lib. 343 of Conv., p. 461.
Cons. $1.

Conveys with other property, "also all the lots and parts of lots of land in the ward aforesaid, which remains of the lands purchased by me of Peter B. Benson and Dr. Van Arsdale, laid down on a map made by J. F. Bridges, City Surveyor, dated 1825, filed in the Register's office, entitled 'Map of the Third Avenue Tract, formerly belonging to P. B. Benson and Dr. Van Arsdale.'"

Benjamin L. Benson,

To

Harriet M. Wiswall.

DEED.
Dated June 2, 1835.
Ackd. June 8th, 1835.
Recd. June 10th, 1835.
Liber 333 of of Conv., p. 258.
Cons.$1.

Conveys with other property.

"All those certain pieces, or parcels of land, marsh, or meadow, partly covered by water, situate, lying and being in the twelfth ward of the City of New York, laid down on said map, but not numbered, and *lying between the First and Fifth Avenues and south of* 107*th Street as far as the said Fifth Avenue tract extends.*"

These deeds include the whole of the Mill Pond. It will be observed that the last recited deed purports to convey "all of the land of the party of the first part, 'lying between the First and the Fifth Avenues, and south of 107th Street.' But it is qualified by the words '*as far as the said Fifth Avenue tract extends*'." As the grantor had no land south of 107 Street and between the *First* and *Third* Avenues, he should have limited the boundary to between the Mill dam and Fifth Avenue.

Neither Benjamin L. Benson nor Peter B. Benson, through whom he derived his title to the Mill Pond, had any land east of the Mill dam and south of 107th Street.

The deed made by Benjamin Benson to his son Peter B. Benson is expressly limited, to "*all my estate on the north side of the Mill Pond*" and it includes "*the Mill Stream, Mill and Mill Pond.*" His clearly expressed intention was to give his son Peter the farm on which he resided, with all its belongings, and nothing more. It had no reference to Mill Creek or Harlem Creek below the dam. The Mill, Mill Stream and Mill Pond had always belonged to that farm from the time he built his dwelling on the north side of the Creek. The words in the deed to Peter B. Benson, "including the mill stream, mill and mill pond," refer to that part of the creek enclosed by the dam. This was not simply a tide mill, it had also the supply of the fresh water streams, of which Harlem Creek was the outlet. The creek behind the dam was the Mill stream. There was a branch on the northerly side of this part of the creek, about three or four hundred feet west of the dam ; it ran about east, being divided by a small island, and a short distance beyond widened into a pond of about an acre. The end of the pond was within a few feet of a cove that led up from the northerly side of the mill creek, between Third and Second

Avenues. A canal was cut to connect this branch and pond with the cove. This formed the mill race. The mill was placed here, the water supplying the mill passed through this branch from the pond, and when it left the mill it passed into the cove and so through the creek to the Harlem River. This branch stream which fed the mill, was no doubt the Mill stream referred to in the deed from Benjamin to Peter B. Benson. The deed is then consistent with the grantor's estate on the northerly side of Mill Pond, namely, the farm, together with mill-stream, mill and mill pond.

> See map of the estate of Margaret McGown, made by Jno. B. Holmes.
> Also the map annexed to the report of the Commission for opening Third Avenue, filed in 1814, which shows this "Mill Stream."

CHAPTER XI.

The Harlem Creek, The Harlem Mill Pond and Van Keulen's Hook.

PART SECOND.

After the erection of the mill and the construction of the dam, by which the creek was divided into two parts of nearly equal length, the part east of the Mill dam ultimately became generally known as Harlem Mill Creek or Benson's Creek, and the division west of the dam as the Mill Pond.

It has been shown that the deed from the magistrates and freeholders of Harlem to Montagne, of Montagne's Point, carried the title to the southerly half of the creek for its whole length to the run of fresh water, and included the southerly half of the Mill Pond; that the deed of the town to Benjamin Benson, of the Mill Camp, included the northerly half of the Mill Pond, and that the deeds of the town for the allotments on Van Keulen's Hook probably included the bed of the northerly half of the creek opposite each lot.

In 1873, the Hon. Murray Hoffman furnished an opinion to Mr. Voorhis, who owned property on the northerly side of the creek between Second and Third Avenues. It involved the question as to the title to Harlem Creek. After a very careful examination of the subject, Judge Hoffman arrived at the conclusion which may be summarized as follows:

That the title to the creek became vested in the freeholders and inhabitants of Harlem by virtue of the Harlem patents.

That the title of the City of New York, under the Dongan Charter, was limited to the strip of land between high and low water mark, at the mouth of the creek measured from point to point.

That the title to the strip of land in question, (part of which was below low water mark on the creek) did pass under the patents, was vested before or in the year 1747 in one claiming under the patents, and that the title was then vested in Mr. Voorhis.

Vide opinion of Judge Hoffman, in full in Appendix F.

That these creeks were of no value to the public as highways of commerce, is further shown by the Acts of the City of New York, in filling them up, and constructing avenues and streets across them by virtue of the power conferred upon it by Statute.

Until within a few years past it seems to have been taken for granted that the individuals who owned land fronting on the respective sides of Harlem Creek, had title to the center of it. There is but little doubt that as a matter of fact that represented the true state of the case.

As to the northerly half of the Creek east of the Milldam, the deeds from the time of the allotments by which the town disposed of Van Keulen's Hook, are missing. That part of the title has to rest on history and tradition.

The City of New York mapped the property and assessed it to the abutting owners, on the streets and avenues, as laid down on the Maps of the city and has awarded damages for the land taken for public use, and assessed the property to individuals for the benefit of the improvements.

It has regularly taxed the property and sold parts of it for non-payment of taxes and assessments. The city has proceeded on the assumption that the owners of the land fronting on the creek, owned to the center of it. In proceedings for opening streets and avenues, the corporation counsels and the Commissioners of Estimate and Assessment ascertain as far as practicable, to whom the land belongs, which is to be condemned and taken for public use, and to whom the awards are to be made for damages.

The fair and reasonable presumption is that the city had *prima facie* evidence as to who these owners were in most cases, and that if the city had owned or claimed the land, that fact would have been known to the officials appointed to look after the interests of the corporation.

The Second Avenue was opened according to law, in 1837, through the McGown Marshes and across the Harlem Mill Creek. The report of the Commissioners of Estimate and Assessment was confirmed April 5, 1837.

> See extracts from the report of the Commissioners in Appendix G.

One Hundred and Seventh Street was opened according to law in 1872, from the Fifth Avenue to the East River. The report of the Commissioners of Estimate and Assessment was filed December 11th, 1872.

> See section from the damage map, with schedule of names of lot owners in Appendix H.

The Town of Harlem ceased to exercise corporate powers some time prior to December 1819. This appears from the petition of the freeholders and inhabitants presented to the Legislature under the date, praying for the appointment of trustees to sell the Harlem Commons. In that petition it was stated there were no persons "then in existence in whom said Common lands could vest."

See Harlem Commons and Louvre, p. 32, also Laws of 1820, Chapter 155.

As far as known, the "freeholders and inhabitants of Harlem" disposed of all of the common or town lands, except the Harlem Commons, before making the above petition to the Legislature. If any such lands remained, the State probably succeeded to the rights of the town. But in the face of the Harlem Patents, no title is presumably in the State. An actual occupant of any land embraced in the Harlem Patents, claiming to be the owner, would, *prima facie*, have derived his title from the town of Harlem. His title may have originated in a grant from the town. In default of a grant, such an occupant may have acquired a good title by adverse possession. When lands have been granted by the sovereignty, there is no presumption in favor of the State, in case of failure of title, aside from proceedings to escheat, as provided by law. The policy of the State is to deal fairly and equitably with actual occupants. This is shown in the laws of 1820, chap. 115, *supra*, in relation to the sale of the Harlem Commons, which contains this saving clause: "Section 2. Provided that nothing herein contained shall be construed to impair, affect or destroy, the legal rights of any person now in possession of any part of such common lands, but that the same shall remain, as before the passage of this act."

This liberal policy of the State is also manifested in its dealings with lands the titles to which are supposed to have failed, from defect of heirs, or alienage, and to have reverted to the people. In cases of this kind the Legislature seldom, if ever, hesitates to pass an act, releasing the claims of the State, whenever it is supposed that injustice might be done to any one, if the escheat is strictly enforced. The acts by which the State releases its interest in such lands, generally contain a provision that nothing in the act shall affect the rights of any heir, devisee or purchaser, or any creditor, by way of mortgage, judgment or otherwise. The State has also always pursued a like liberal and just policy in regard to littoral and riparian proprietors. By the Revised Statutes, the Commissioners of the land office, are empowered " to grant so much of the lands under the waters of navigable rivers or lakes, as they shall deem necessary, to promote the commerce of this State"; and it provides that, "no such grant shall be made to any person other than the proprietor of the adjacent lands," and that "every such grant that shall be made to any other person shall be void."

Revised Statues, C. 9, Title 5, Art. 4, section 67.

If it should be conceded that the Harlem Creeks were *prima facie* public navigable waters, then it would be but reasonable to assume, that the adjacent proprietors had the usual pre-emptive rights to grants of the soil under the waters of the creeks.

CHAPTER XII.

SUMMARY.

All the right, title and interest of the sovereign in the Harlem Creeks was included in the first patent granted by Governor Nicolls to the freeholders and inhabitants of Harlem. The grant included the bed of the creeks down to the ordinary high water line along the shore of the Harlem River and East River.

These creeks were not navigable waters, according to the legal meaning of the term. What navigability they possessed was so limited and unimportant as to be of no value to the public for commercial purposes.

The grant of the creeks was absolute, and it has never been modified or revoked.

These creeks were *prima facie* private waters, and the title of the proprietors of land bordering upon them extended by presumption to the *filum aquæ* of the respective streams.

The title to the southerly half of the Harlem Mill Creek was possessed by John Montagne, and that part east of the mill-dam passed by a complete chain to Margaret McGown. The remainder of the southerly half west of the mill-dam passed by a like chain to Peter B. Benson.

The title to so much of the northerly half of the creek as was west of the mill-dam was conveyed by the Town of Harlem to Benjamin Benson, as a part of the Mill Camp property. Although the deed is missing, the historic evidence of Benson's title is so reliable, and the possession under it so ancient and well authenticated, that the title of Peter B. Benson to the whole of the Mill Pond may, with propriety, be called perfect.

The title to the remainder of the northerly half of the creek eastward of the mill-dam was included in Van Keulen's Hook farm, which was owned by the freeholders and inhabitants of Harlem.

In the allotments and divisions of the farm among the freeholders entitled to participate, the property was disposed of in lots numbered consecutively and fronting on the creek. It is assumed that the descriptions carried the titles to the centre of the creek. The deed from Simon Johnson to Benjamin Benson probably followed the deeds given by the town, and that description goes to the centre of the creek.

As the southerly half of that creek was owned by the Montagnes, father and son, and as the allotments of the Van Keulen's Hook farm were made for agricultural purposes, there was no reason for reserving the bed of the stream opposite the respective lots. The presumption is that the town parted with all its title to the adjoining proprietors or occupiers, and that their titles originated in grants which have been worn out or lost. The most reasonable and probable conclusion is, that Benjamin Benson had a good title to the northerly half of that part of the creek opposite his farm, and that it passed under his deed to his son, Peter B. Benson, and that the title as derived under that deed is good.

APPENDIX A.

King Charles the Second's Grant of New Netherland, Etc., to the Duke of York.

Charles the Second by the Grace of God, King of England, Scotland, France and Ireland, Defender of the Faith, &c. To all to whom these presents shall come greeting: Know ye that we for divers good causes and considerations us thereunto moving have of our especial Grace, certain knowledge and mere motion given and granted by these presents for us our heirs and successors do give and grant unto our dearest brother James, Duke of York, his heirs and assigns, All that part of the main land of New England beginning at a certain place called or known by the name St. Croix next adjoining to New Scotland in America and from thence extending along the Sea Coast unto a certain place called Petauquine and so up the River thereof to the furthest head of the same as it tendeth Northward; and extending from thence to the River Kinebequi and so upwards by the shortest course to the River Canada Northward. And also all that Island or Islands commonly called by the several name or names of Matowacks or Long Island situate lying and being towards the West of Cape Cod and the narrow Higansetts abutting upon the main land between the two Rivers there called or known by the several names of Connecticut and Hudson's River together also with the said River called Hudson's River and all the land from the west side of Connecticut to the East side of Delaware Bay. And also all those several Islands called and known by the names of Martin's Vineyard and Nautukes otherwise Nautuckett; Together with all the Lands, Islands, Soils, Rivers, Harbors, Mines, Minerals, Quarries, Woods, Marshes, Waters, Lakes, Fishings, Hawking, Hunting and Fowling and all other Royalties, Profits, Commodities and Hereditaments to the said several Islands, Lands and Premises belonging and appertaining with their and every of their appurtenances; and all our Estate, Right, Title, Interest,

Benefit, Advantage, Claim and Demand of, in and to the
said lands and premises or any part or parcel thereof and
the reversion and reversions, remainder and remainders
together with the yearly and other rents, Revenues and
Profits of and singular the said premises and every part
and parcel thereof; to have and to hold all and singular
the said lands islands, hereditaments and premises with
their and every of their appurtenances hereby given and
granted or hereinbefore mentioned to be given and granted
unto our Dearest Brother James, Duke of York, his heirs
and assigns forever to the only proper use and behoof of
the said James Duke of York, his heirs and assigns forever,
to be holden of us, our heirs and successors as of our manor
of East Greenwich and our County of Kent in free and
common soccage and not in Capite nor by Knight service
yielding and rendering. And the said James Duke of York
doth for himself, his heirs and assigns covenant and promise to yield and render unto us our heirs and successors of
and for the same yearly and every year forty Beaver skins
when they shall be demanded or within Ninety days after.
And we do further of our special Grace certain knowledge
and mere motion for us our heirs and successors give and
Grant unto our said Dearest Brother James, Duke of York,
his heirs, Deputies, Agents Commissioners and Assigns by
these presents full and absolute power and authority to
correct, punish, pardon, govern and rule all such the subjects of Our heirs and successors who may from time to time
adventure themselves into any of the parts or places aforesaid or that shall or do at any time hereafter inhabit within
the same according to such laws, Orders, Ordinance, Directions and Instruments as by our said Dearest Brother or
his assigns shall be established; and in defect thereof in
case of necessity, according to the good discretion of his
Deputies, Commissioners, Officers or Assigns, respectively;
as well in all causes and matters Capital and Criminal as
civil both marine and others; so always as the said Statutes, Ordinances and proceedings be not contrary to but
as near as conveniently may be agreeable to the Laws, Statutes and Government of this Our Realm of England, and

saving and reserving to us our Heirs and successors the receiving, hearing and determining of the Appeal and Appeals of all of any person or persons of in or belonging to the territories or Islands aforesaid in or touching any Judgment or Sentence to be there made or given. And further that it shall and may be lawful to and for our said Dearest Brother his heirs and assigns by these presents from time to time to nominate, make, constitute, ordain and confirm by such name or names, stile or stiles as to him or them shall seem good, and likewise to revoke, discharge, change and alter as well all and singular, Governors, Officers and Ministers which hereafter shall be by him or them thought fit and needful to be made or used within the aforesaid parts and Islands; and also to make, ordain and establish all manner of Orders, Laws, directions, instructions, forms and ceremonies of Government and Magistracy fit and necessary for and concerning the Government of the territories and Islands aforesaid, so always as the same be not contrary to the laws and statutes of this Our Realm of England; but as near as may be agreeable thereunto: And the same at all times hereafter to put in execution or abrogate, revoke or change not only within the precincts of the said Territories or Islands but also upon the seas in going and coming to and from the same as he or they in their good discretions shall think to be fittest for the good of the adventurers and Inhabitants there, and we do further of our special Grace, certain knowledge and mere motion grant, ordain and declare that such Governors, Officers and Ministers as shall from time to time be authorized and appointed in manner and form aforesaid shall and may have full power and authority to use and exercise Martial Law in cases of rebellion, insurrection and mutiny in as large and ample manner as Our Lieutenants in Our counties within Our Realm of England have or ought to have by force of their Commission of Lieutenancy or any Law or Statute of this Our Realm. And We do further by these presents for us Our heirs and successors, grant unto our said Dearest Brother James, Duke of York, his heirs and assigns, that it shall and may be lawful to and for the said

James, Duke of York, his heirs and assigns in his or their
discretion from time to time to admit such and so many
person or persons to trade and traffic unto and within the
territories and islands aforesaid and into every or any part
and parcel thereof, and to have, possess, and enjoy any
Lands and Hereditaments in the parts and places aforesaid
as they shall think fit according to the Laws, Orders, Constitutions and Ordinances of Our said Brother, his heirs,
Deputies, Commissioners, and assigns from time to time to
be made and established by virtue of and according to
the true intent and meaning of these presents and under
such conditions, reservations, and agreements as Our said
Brother, his heirs or assigns shall set down, order, direct
and appoint and not otherwise as aforesaid, and we do further of Our especial Grace, certain knowledge and mere
motion for us our heirs and successors give and grant to
our said Dear Brother his heirs and assigns by these presents, that it shall and may be lawful to and for him, them
or any of them at all and every time and times hereafter
out of any Our Realm or Dominions whatsoever to take,
lead, carry and transport in and into their voyages and for
and towards the Plantations of Our said Territories and
Islands all such and so many of Our loving subjects or any
other strangers being not prohibited or under restraint that
will become Our Loving subjects and live under Our allegiance as shall willingly accompany them in the said voyages together with all such clothing, implements, furniture,
and other things usually transported and not prohibited as
shall be necessary for the inhabitants of the said Islands
and Territories and for their use and defence thereof and
managing and carrying on the trade with the People there
and in passing and returning to and fro: Yielding and
paying to us, Our Heirs and successors, the Customs and
Duties therefore due and payable according to the Laws and
customs of this Our Realm. And we do also for us Our
Heirs and successors, grant to Our said Dearest Brother,
James Duke of York, his heirs and assigns and to all and
every such Governor or Governors or other officers or Ministers as by Our said Brother his heirs or assigns shall be

appointed, to have power and authority of Government and Command in or over the inhabitants of the said Territories or Islands that they and every of them shall and lawfully may from time to time and at all times hereafter forever for their several defence and safety encounter, expulse, repel and resist by force of Arms as well by sea as by land and all ways and means whatsoever all such person and persons as without the special License of Our said Dear Brother his heirs or assigns shall attempt to inhabit within the several precincts and limits of Our said territories and Islands: and also all and every such person and persons whatsover as shall enterprize or attempt at any time hereafter the destruction, invasion, detriment or annoyance to the parts, places or Islands aforesaid or any part thereof. And lastly our will and pleasure is, and we do hereby declare and grant, that these Our Letters Patents or the enrolment thereof shall be good and effectual in the law to all intents and purposes, whatsoever notwithstanding the not reciting or mentioning of the premises or any part thereof, or the meets or bounds thereof, or of any former or other Letters Patents or Grants heretofore made or granted of the premises, or of any part thereof by us or of any of our progenitors unto any other person or persons whatsoever, bodies Politic or Corporate, or any Act, Law or other restraint incertainty or imperfection whatsoever to the contrary in any wise notwithstanding; although express mention of the true yearly value or certainty of the premises, or any of them, or any other gifts or grants by us or by any of our progenitors or predecessors heretofore made to the said James, Duke of York, in these presents is not made, or any statute, act, ordinance, provision, proclamation or restriction heretofore had, made, enacted, ordained or provided, or any other matter, cause or thing, whatsoever to the contrary thereof in anywise notwithstanding.

In Witness Whereof we have caused these, Our Letters, to be made Patents, Witness Ourself at Westminster the twelfth day of March in the sixteenth year of our reign. (1664).

By the king.   Howard.

Original in State Library, Albany: Patents I, 109-115
Leaming and Spicer, 3-8; New York Colonial Documents,
II, 295-298.

Brodhead's History of the State of New York II.,
651-652.

The Duke of York's Commission to Colonel Richard Nicolls.

James, Duke of York and Albany, Earl of Ulster, Lord
High Admiral of England and Ireland, etc., Constable of
Dover Castle, Lord Warden of the Cinque Ports and Governor of Portsmouth, etc. Whereas it hath pleased the King's
Most Excellent Majesty, my Sovereign Lord and Brother,
by His Majesty's Letters Patents, bearing date at Westminster the twelfth day of March in the sixteenth year of
his Majesty's Reign, to give and grant unto me and to my
heirs and assigns, All that part of the mainland of New
England, Beginning at a certain place called or known by
the name of Saint Croix, next adjoining to New Scotland in
America, and from thence extending along the sea coast,
into a certain place called Petaquine and so up the River
thereof to the furthest head of the same, as it tendeth
Northwards, and extending from thence to the River of
Kinebequi, and so upwards by the shortest course to the
River Canada Northwards, And also all that Island or
Islands commonly called by the several names or names of
Matowacks or Long Island, situate, lying and being towards
the west of Cape Cod and the Narrow-Higansets, abutting
upon the mainland, between the two rivers there called or
known by the several names of Connecticut and Hudson's
River; Together also with the said River called Hudson's
River and all the lands from the West side of Connecticut
River to the East side of Delaware Bay; And also all those
several Islands called or known by the name of Martin's
Vineyard and Nantukes otherwise Nantucket; Together
with all the Lands, Islands, Soils, Rivers, Harbors, Mines,
Minerals, Quarries, Woods, Marshes, Lakes, Fishing,

Hawking, Hunting and Fowling, and all other Royalties, Profits, Commodities, Hereditaments, to the said several Islands, Lands and premises belonging and appertaining, with their and every of their appurtenances; to Hold the same to my own proper use and behoof with power to correct, punish, pardon, govern and Rule the inhabitants thereof, by myself, or such Deputies, Commissioners or Officers as I shall think fit to appoint; as by His Majesty's said Letters Patents may more fully appear; and Whereas I have conceived a good opinion of the Integrity, Prudence, Ability and Fitness of Richard Nicolls, Esquire, to be employed as my Deputy there, I have therefore thought fit to constitute and appoint, and I do hereby constitute and appoint him the said Richard Nicolls, Esquire, to be my Deputy-Governor within the lands, Islands and places aforesaid, To perform and execute all and every the Powers which are by the said Letters Patents granted unto me to be executed by my Deputy, Agent or assign, to have and to Hold the said place of Deputy-Governor unto the said Richard Nicolls, Esquire, during my will and pleasure only; Hereby willing and requiring all and every the Inhabitants of the said Lands, Islands and Places to give obedience to him the said Richard Nicolls in all things, according to the tenor of his Majesty's said Letters Patents; And the said Richard Nicolls, Esquire, to observe, follow, and execute such Orders and Instructions as he shall from time to time receive from myself. Given under my hand and seal at Whitehall, this second day of April, in the sixteenth year of the Reign of Our Sovereign Lord Charles the Second, by the Grace of God, King of England, Scotland and Ireland etc., *Annoque Domini*, 1664.

James.

By Command of His Royal Highness, W. Coventry.

Patents I. 116-118; Leaming and Spicer 665-667.
Brodhead's History of the State of New York, Vol II. 653.

APPENDIX B, No. 1.

Agreement between John Montagne and John Louwe Bogert for the sale of Montagne's Point or Rechcowanis and the Meadows in the Bay of Hellgate.

On this day the 18th May 1671, appeared before me Jan de Lamontagne, Secretary of this town admitted by the High and Honorabe Mayor's Court, Jan Lamontagne, aforesaid and Jan Louwe Van Schoonderwoert*, the which acknowledge to have bargained with one another about the sale of a piece of land named in the Dutch language Montagne's Point, or by the Indians Rechcowanis, on condition as follows: Firstly, Jan Lamontagne aforesaid constitutes himself as seller, and Jan Louwe Van Schoonderwoert as the buyer of the aforesaid point, with the meadows lying in the Bend of Hellgate, which the seller has received in exchange for the Town lot's meadows ; The point is bounded between two creeks up to the hill, and behind by a hill, with the meadows which are annexed, and all that on it is fast by earth and nails, excepting the sowing of grain and the plants of the hop plantation, with apple and pear trees, and twelve cherry trees, which the seller reserves to himself; and that for the sum of three thousand guilders in sewant, or in grain at the price of sewant, without allowing the buyer to shift himself to any other payment, renouncing the benefit of every other pay ; and that on the next coming first of May, Anno 1672, the first payment, being fifteen hundred guilders, shall be made in payment as is aforesaid, the other half one year after date, in the before named payment, being also fifteen hundred guilders ; the seller promises this aforesaid land, with the meadows, for the before named sum, to deliver free and unincumbered when the first payment shall be paid (saving the right of the lord) ; provided that the buyer shall give a bond for the remaining payment ; also agreed that the seller shall remain

---

* The same person who is afterwards called *Jan Louwe Bogert*. Translator.

in possession until the first payment shall become due and be paid; the buyer is at liberty to enter upon the unoccupied land immediately, and the other land as the harvest is taken off; the risk shall run at the charge of the buyer, except where it may arise through the negligence of the seller; the seller promises to harrow the piece by the cherry trees once. The above written we the buyer and seller promise to keep and fulfill, in the presence of Meyndert Maljaart and Dirck Cornelissen, as witnesses hereunto requested. Dated as above, in the jurisdiction of N. Haarlem.

         J. Lamontagne,
         Jaan Van Sooderwoer.

This ⊘ is the mark of
Meynder Naljaart.
Dierck Cornelissen Hoochlandt.

         Translated by me,
         James Riker.

APPENDIX B, No. 2.

Deed from the Magistrates of Harlem to John Montagne for Montagne's Point and the Meadows in the Bay of Hellgate.

We, the Honorable Magistrates, with the vote and resolution of the Inhabitants of this town, have granted forever and as hereditary, to Jan de La Montagne, a piece of land, with the meadows thereto annexed, named Montagne's Point, formerly possessed by his late father, lying within our town's jurisdiction, bounded on the North side by a creek called Montagne's Kill; extending from the East River unto a little fresh-water creek running between Montagne's Flat and aforesaid Point; on the South side bounded by a creek and a meadow and by hills, to the aforesaid little fresh-water creek where the King's Majesty his highway, goes over; with the Meadows lying in the bend of Hellgate, which Montagne beforenamed has had in exchange for the Town Lot's meadows; with such rights and privileges as are granted us by patent and still remain to grant; provided he submit to such laws and servitudes as with us are common and may be imposed, without that we or our Inhabitants, now or in future days, shall have any claim thereupon; but as his other patrimonial property may enter upon and use or sell, as he may resolve and shall choose, saving the lord's right. For further security, and that our deed shall have greater force and legal authority, we the Magistrates and Constable subscribe the same, this 8th February, *Anno.* 1672, in New Haerlem.

       D. TOURNEUR,
       RESALVERT WALDRON,
       JOHANNES VERMELJE,
       DAVID DES MAREST,
       PIETER ROELOFSEN, *Constable.*

Translated by me,
    JAMES RIKER.

APPENDIX B, No. 3.

Resolution of the Constable and Magistrates Estimating the Land of Bogert Purchased from La Montagne at 18 morgen.

Anno 167 ⅔, the 16th January.

It is resolved by the Constable and Magistrates, to estimate the land possessed by Jan Laurens* Van Schoonrewoert, successor of Jan Lamontagne, at 18 *morgen.*

    Present: DAVID DES MAREST,
       JOOST VAN OBLINUS,
       GLAUDE LE MAISTRE,
       LUBBERT GERRITSEN,
       CORNELIS JANSEN, *Constable.*

 By order of the same,
      HENDR. J. VANDR. VIN,
          Secretary.

Translated by me,
    JAMES RIKER.

---

* Laurens and Louwe were the same name. Trans.

APPENDIX B, No. 4.

Deed for the Hop Garden by Maria Vermilje, Widow of Jan de La Montagne, to Cornelia Everts, Wife of Jan Louwe Van Schoonrewoert (or Bogert).

Appeared before me Hendrick J. Van der Vin, Secretary, residing at the village of New Haerlem, and the after-named witnesses, the modest Maria Vermilje, widow of the deceased Jan de Lamontagne, on the one, and Cornelia Everts, at present the wife of Jan Louwe Van Schoonrewoert, as authorized by her husband, on the other side, who acknowledged with one another to have agreed as follows: Maria Vermilje has sold to the aforesaid Cornelia her hop garden, lying behind the land of the aforesaid Jan Louwe against the hills; with all the rights and dependencies thereof, which she the seller was having; for three hundred guilders, of which sum she acknowledges to be paid in full the last penny with the first; therefore the said hop garden cedes and conveys to the said Jan Louwe Van Schoonrewoert, in free and lawful ownership, without she, the seller, reserving or pretending any claim thereto, but letting the buyer do therewith as his own good will shall decide; promising this conveyance to free and indemnify against every one who shall bring any action or be disposed to make any pretense to the said Hop garden, saving the lord his right, without craft or design, under obligation according to the laws. Thus done and executed at New Haerlem, in the presence of Daniel Tourneur and Thomas Holland, as witnesses hereto requested, who with the appearers and me the secretary have there undersigned, this 4th November *Anno* 1679.

Maria Vermelje
her
Cornelia X Everts. *
mark

Daniel Tourneur,
his
Thomas H Holland,
mark.

* Called by their maiden names, as was then the custom.

In presence of me,

Hendr. J. Vandr. Vin,
Secretary.

Translated by me,

James Riker.
Trans.

APPENDIX B, No. 5.

Judgment in Joost Van Oblinus v. Jan Louwe Bogert relating to a small meadow in Southerly end of the Bay of Hellgate.

Thursday, this date 4th December 1679.

All present, the old and new magistrates,

Resolved Waldron
Jan Dyckman
Laurens Jansen
Arent Hermensen (Bussing)
Jan Hendricks (Brevoort)
Johannes Vermelje
Joost Van Oblinus
Daniel Tourneur

Joost Van Oblinus, Pltf.

v.

Jan Louwe.

Whereas a dispute has arisen between Joost van Oblinus and Jan Louwe van Schoonrewoert over a certain small meadow lying in the Bend of Hellgate, which each of the parties claims as belonging to him; after several debates and rebuts on either side, it was decided by the Honorable Court, (the said small meadow being the most southerly in the range under against the steep hill next the little kil,) that Jan Louwe for his meadows shall have those that stretch from his great kil to the little kil from anckers house; the rest to Joost van Oblinus. And ordered that each shall bear his own costs attaching to this case.

Translated by me,
James Riker.

APPENDIX B, No. 6.

Deed of the Overseers and Authorized men of Harlem to Jan Louwe Bogert for a piece of land lying in the Bend of Hell Gate. Being lot No 25 of common lands.

On this date the 2d May 1700;

Meeting held at the village of N. Haarlem.

Present the Overseers and Authorized, Louwerens Jansen, Pieter van Oblinis, Jaques Tourneur, and Arent Harmensen, Adolph Meyer, Samuel Waldron.

By order of Adolph Meyer, Jan Hendricksen Brevoort, Pieter van Oblinis and Samuel Waldron, authorized by the community at N. Haarlem, as appears from the proceedings of 29th November and the 11th December 1691, there was measured out for the undernamed person the following land. And thereupon the overseers and authorized have had written the following deed, such as they were also empowered to make, upon the 14th December 1699.

There is set off for Jan Louwe Boogert (for the right of 16 morgen of land and one *erf* right), a piece of land lying in the Bend of Hellgate, Beginning, from the southwest corner of the Hop Garden, by a birch tree, till to a white oak tree which stands by a little swamp, marked J. L. B. and J. D. L., thence towards the river past a rock marked J. L. B. and J. D. L., and so onward to the shore till to the end of a meadow north of a rocky hill; as it is at present fenced in. Signed the 21st March 1701.

Pieter van Oblinis ⎫
                     his ⎪
Jaques Tourneur ST ⎬ Overseers.
                mark ⎪
                his ⎪
Louwerens Jansen + ⎪
                mark ⎭

Samuel Waldron ⎫
Pieter van Oblinis ⎪
Arent H. Bussing ⎪
            his ⎪
Adolph Meyer AM ⎪
           mark ⎬ Authorized.
            his ⎪
Jaques Tourneur ST ⎪
               mark ⎪
            his ⎪
Louwerens Jansen + ⎪
              mark ⎭

                          Adr. Vermenle
                                  Clerk.
                Translated by me,
                        James Riker.

APPENDIX B, No. 7.

Deed of the Overseers and Authorized Men of Harlem to Jan de Lamaeter, for a Piece of Land lying in the Bend of Hell Gate, Being lot No. 26 of common lands.

On this date, the 2d May, 1700:
Meeting held at the village N. Haarlem.

Present the Overseers and the Authorized men, Louwerens Jansen, Pieter v: Oblienis, Jaques Tourneur and Arent Har. Bussing, Adolph Meyer, Samuel Waldron.

By order of Adolph Meyer, Jan Hendricksen van Brevoort, Pieter van Oblienis and Samuel Waldron authorized by the community of New Haarlem, as appears from the proceedings of 29th November and the 11th December 1691, there was measured out for the undernamed person the following land. And thereupon the overseers and authorized have had written the following deed, such as they were also empowered to make, upon the 14th December, 1699.

There is set off to Jan de Lamaeter for nine morgen of land and one erf right, a piece of land lying in the Bend of Hellgate, extending from the Northwest corner of the end of his lots to a white oak tree marked J. D. L. and J. L. B., thence towards the river past a rock marked J. D. L. and J. L. B., and so onward to the shore, till to the end of the meadow north of a rocky hill. Signed the 21st March, 1701.

Peter V. Oblinis
Jaques Tourneur his ST mark   ⎫
Louwerens Jansen his + mark   ⎬ Overseers.

Samuel Waldron
Pieter v. Oblinis
Arent Har. Bussing
Jaques Tourneur his ST mark   ⎫
Adolph Meyer his AM mark   ⎬ Authorized.
Louwerens Jansen his + mark

Adr. Vermenle, Clerk.

Translated by me,
James Riker.

APPENDIX B, No. 8.

Minutes of the Town of Harlem dated January 3d, 1667, Relative to Building the Dam for Delavall's Mill at Harlem Creek.

On this date, 3d January, *Ao.* 1667, the Honorable Mr. Delavall proposed and requested that the magistrates of this town do consider the following points:

*   *   *

3d. That it be firmly settled that the inhabitants of the town will make the dam; because other towns promise to make a dam if it should please him to build the mill near them.

4th. Requests leave to erect a stone house at the rear of his land near the mill, and to fortify it, as a refuge for the village in time of need.

5th. Requests leave to run a fence straight from the fence now standing to the stone bridge upon Van Keulen's Hook, and to use the land and meadows inclosed.

*   *   *

On the 4th of January: Advice of the inhabitants of the town upon the propositions of the Hon. Mr. Delavall:

*   *   *

3d. Agree to make the dam for the mill, provided they may enjoy its benefits according to custom.

4th. Agree that a house or bouwery may be rebuilt, to set near the mill, or where is most convenient for him.

5th. Agree that the mill have the use of the land and meadow lying from the fence now standing to the stone bridge on Van Keulen's Hook.

*   *   *

Translated by me,
James Riker.

APPENDIX B, No. 9.

Deed for Mrs. Maria Vermilje, the widow of John Montagne, to John Louwe Bogert for Montagne's Point and the Meadows in the Bay of Hellgate.

Appeared before me Hendrick Jansen Vander Vin, Secretary of the Town of New Harlem, and the afternamed witnesses, Mrs. Maria Vermilje, the widow of Jan de la Montainje, late Secretary of this town, who in his life-time has sold to Jan Louwe Van Schoonderwort his piece of land called Montainje's Point, together with the meadows thereunto belonging, as shown by an article of the sale thereof dated 18 May, 1671, and by indenture bearing date 8 February, 1672, for the sum of three thousand guilders, of which sum the appearer, characterized as above, hereby acknowledges the receipt in full to the last penny, in the first place giving thanks to the buyer for his punctuality, and releasing him from all future demands. Therefore as it has been ceded and conveyed, so the grantor hereby cedes and conveys the said piece of land, and meadows thereunto belonging, to him the buyer, in free and true possession, as they were possessed by her, without that she the appearer, or her heirs, thereto shall claim any right; putting him the said buyer into the right and actual possession of the same, without doing or permitting anything against the same; promising always to clear and defend this conveyance; to indemnify him and keep him harmless from cost and damage against every one that may or shall bring claim or pretension to the same (all this without art or cunning): To the fulfillment of this and what is before written the appearer binds herself and her property, personal and real, without any exception. The appearer acknowledges the truth of this by her own hand underwritten; in presence of Mr. David des Marest (ruling magistrate) and Dan. Tourneur, as witnesses hereto besought

and requested. Thus done and executed at New Harlem on the 30th Day of the month of March, 1674.
Maria Montainje.
Witnesses:
David des Marest,
Daniel Tourneur.
Hendrick Jans. Vander Vin,
Secretary.

Extract out of the Register of New Harlem.

APPENDIX B, No. 10.

Historical statement of James Riker Esq relative to lots Nos 21, 22. 23 and other lots on Van Keulen's Hook and Jockem Pieters tract &c

Mem. by James Riker.

[The mill was built; being referred to in 1668, '69, '73, &c., and also so stated in Capt. Delavall's deed to Carteret in 1676.

As to the allotment of No. 22 Van Keulen's Hook to John LeRoy, his tranfer to Moesman and his to Delavall; and the laying out of lot 23 to Delavall, to take the place of No. 21, the following facts appear.

In the list of the allotments on Van Keulen's Hook, made out in 1662, the names of the grantees were entered opposite the several numbers up to and including No. 21. But the space opposite lot 22 was left blank for the reason I presume, that just then LeRoy, who had "contracted" to buy out Philip Presto's allotment (which included a lot on Jochem Pieters), was having a dispute with Presto, in Court, over their bargain. It was settled, and LeRoy got Presto's land; with the lot 22, as appears by an original description of lot 21, in which he is named as adjoining owner on the west side.

The lot on Jochem Pieters which LeRoy got of Presto, is shown to have been one of the three numbers 20, 21, 22.

This is a logical inference from the fact that, while it was one of the Jochem Pieters lots, it was not any one of the other 19 lots, the history of which is clearly traced. It further appears that within a short time, Moesman came to Harlem, (in 1663), and became the owner of two of the three aforesaid lots on Jochem Pieters, prior to March 13. 1664, while somewhere about the same time (previous, we infer, to Dec. 27. 1663) LeRoy sold his two Presto lots, having bought another allotment June 1. 1662, nearer the village, and which he occupied many years. That near the close of 1664, Moesman returned to Holland, when Delavall appears as owner of the Presto lots, No. 22 V. K. Hook, and one of the Nos. 20–22, J. P. Flat. The third lot of these three (not owned by Moesman) is quite satisfactorily traced from Adam Dircksen, through Morris Peterson and Valentine Claessen to Delavall. We place Moesman's two lots on Jochem Pieters within the three numbers 20–22, for the same reason before given that the exact knowledge we have of the other 19 lots makes it clear that his two lots were not among them. But Delavall's testimony in the deed of 1676, shows that we need not go to find the Moesman lots outside of those he then conveyed to Carteret. From all this I think we must conclude that in Moesman's two allotments (an allotment then embraced a farm lot on Jochem Pieters, a *supplementary* lot on Van Keulen's Hook, a house lot, garden and salt meadows; and these were rarely sold separately at that early date), were included LeRoy's lot 22 on Van Keulen's Hook and his lot on J. P. Flat.

When Delavall in his deed to Carteret, in 1676, conveys the farm he "formerly bought of one Moseman," that description was understood as carrying the six of the lots belonging to him on Jochem Pieters *which lay in one tract*, although but two of those lots were actually bought of Moesman; and therefore the inexact language of that deed is not to be taken as showing that lot No. 22 Van Keulen's Hook was not also a part of the Moesman farm, against the evidence that it was.

The facts in brief might be thus stated: John LeRoy

became possessed of lot No. 22 Van Keulen's Hook under the allotment of 1662, and as a supplementary grant to a lot on Jochem Pieters (one of the Nos. 20, 21, 22) which he had purchased of Philip Presto. Arent Moesman buying in 1663, two of the said three lots, together with their supplementary lots on Van Keulen's Hook, thus came to own the lot 22 first above named, and which in 1664, he conveyed with the rest of his two allotments to Thomas Delavall.

Delavall, by an exchange of lots with Glaude Delamater in 1673, came in possession of No. 21, Van Keulen's Hook, which Delamater had purchased prior to 1668, when he had it patented. But for some reason (and facts seem to point to a very good one), after Delamater's death, his widow laid claim to this lot 21, and on June 4. 1690 sold it to her son in law Arent Bussing, who continued to hold it. To get over the difficulty Delavall was granted another lot on the west side of 22, and which was done prior to June 29, 1691, (when John Delavall was in possession of the two lots) and I think before the sale of lot 21 to Bussing.

I have never met with the assignment from Elias Pipon to Simon Johnson and others, but it is recited in an original deed dated Sept. 25. 1747, of which the following is the preamble.

"Whereas I, Simon Johnson, John Auboyneau and James Favieres (the two last late of the City of New York, merchants, deceased) three of the creditors of Elias Pipon, Being by divers mean conveyances seized in fee of all the lands which lately were of the said Elias Pipon, in trust that we by sale of the premises might raise sufficient for the payment of the debts of the said Elias Pipon and return to him the overplus," &c.

The same facts are stated in a petition of Johnson, Auboyneau and Faviere to the Gov. and Council Apl. 6. 1737. (N. Y. Council Minutes.) Also in printed N. Y. Assembly Journals of Apl. 20. 1737.

APPENDIX B, No. 11.

Minutes of the Town of Harlem of October 23, 1738, containing grant to Samson Benson to build a dam and a mill on the Mill Camp, "in place of Delavall's Mill gone to decay."

On this date, the 23d October, in the year 1738, the inhabitants and Owners of New Haarlem, by their signatures underwritten, have consented and agreed with Samson Benson, in regard to the setting or building of a Mill with a dam on the Mill Creek, on the following conditions: The inhabitants and the owners of New Haarlem, who have signed this writing do give permission to the said Samson Benson to set a Mill with a dam on the Mill Camp wherever it may suit him best, and that for him and his heirs; and for the making or repairing the dam may draw stones and earth in the Mill Camp as if it were his own; and the undersigned promise in all uprightness that neither they nor their heirs or successors, nor any of them will ever disturb him in respect to shutting of the dam on the said creek, or their right to the creek, which the undersigned for themselves, their heirs and successors fully give to the said Samson Benson, and that upon condition that the said Samson Benson shall honestly perform the following:

First, that after the Mill shall have been built, and it shall get out of repair, and shall remain useless for two years, the right to the creek shall revert to the town again.

Second, that the said Samson Benson shall be bound to provide that the neighbors suffer no damage to their meadows.

Third, that the inhabitants of New Haarlem shall have the freedom of fishing, shooting and oystering in the creek as before.

Fourth, that the inhabitants of New Haarlem who have signed this, and their successors, shall have the first privilege, before the outside people, whether bakers, bolters or farmers, to wit, two days of the week as Tuesdays and Saturdays. **Done at New Haarlem,** on the date as above.

     her
Maria × Meyer
     mark
Pieter Van Oblinis,
     his
Dirck DB Benson.
     mark
Johannes Waldron
Johannes Benson
Johannes Meyer
Barent Waldron
Abram Meyer
     his
Lourens + Low
     mark
Arent Bussing
Jan Kiersen
Jan Dykman
Jacob Dyckman
Wilhelmus Waldron
Adolph Meyer
Jan Nagel
Johannes Waldron.

This is signed, sealed and delivered in the presence of us,
  Harmen Vandewater, } as witnesses.
  Elbert Haring,
     Translated by me,
       James Riker.

APPENDIX B, No. 12.

Award of Lewis Morris of the Manor of Morrisania, Abraham Van Wyck and others on behalf of the freeholders of the township of New Harlem, allotting the Mill Camp Tract adjoining the Mill Pond to Bnejamin Benson.

To all Christian People, to whom this present writing of Award Indented shall come, We, Lewis Morris, of the Manor of Morrisania, in the County of Westchester, Esqr.

Abraham Van Wyck and Abraham Lefferts, of the City of New York, Merchants, Send Greeting: Whereas the freeholders of the township of New Harlem, at a town meeting held in the said town on the twentieth day of December, one thousand seven hundred and fifty two, did by plurality of voices, nominate and appoint us Arbitrators to settle, adjust and determine the several disputes and differences that had from time to time subsisted and still did subsist between the said freeholders concerning their several rights in the patent of New Harlem, and also all other disputes whatsoever that had arisen concerning their several public transactions of their town in laying out their commons, or selling of any of their lands, . . . Now know Ye, that we the said arbitrators . . have, and by these presents do unanimously make, publish and declare this our Award, order, judgment and final determination of and upon the premises aforesaid in the manner and form following, that is to say: . . . Whereas Benjamin Benson, one other of the said freeholders has a grant from the said town of New Harlem for liberty of using stone and earth from and out of the Mill Camp within the bounds of the said town, for the use of his mill dam, and being willing to have the said Mill Camp assured and conveyed to him and his heirs forever for a reasonable consideration, We therefore having taken into consideration his claim of privilege, do award, order and adjudge that he pay or cause to be paid to the said elders and deacons the sum of One hundred and sixty pounds current money aforesaid for the absolute purchase thereof, and that within three months after the date hereof; and that a deed be made and executed to him and his heirs for the same by and according to the bounds and limits following, to wit: Beginning at the fence of the said Benjamin Benson by the Mill Creek and runs along his fence Northwardly to Harlem road about thirty one chains, thence along said road twenty three chains and one half, which is three chains beyond a large oak tree near Van Breemen's house, thence south ten degrees east to the said Mill Creek, thence along the said Creek to the place where it began; in which deed shall be contained a covenant or proviso that the said Benjamin Benson, his heirs and assigns whom shall be owner and owners of the said Mill for the time being shall at all times and forever leave and keep a convenient road, with a swinging gate, for passing and repassing over the Mill Camp to the said mill, and that the same deed be made and executed in the same manner as hath been used by the said freeholders on the sale of their said common lands; and we do also award and order that when and so soon as the said consideration money is paid and deed executed, they the said freeholders shall be thenceforward fully and absolutely acquitted and discharged of and from all demands whatsoever from the said Benjamin Benson on pretence of any moneys by him paid for their use on any suit or suits in law or otherwise for or in respect of the defense of the title to the said Mill Camp, in anywise; We so also award order and adjudge that no encroachments shall be made from the westermost limits of this grant to Benjamin Benson, but that the small part of the Mill Camp which remains undisposed of, lying between his westermost bounds and the Mill Creek, so far as the bridge, shall be and remain in common free and open for the benefit of all the freeholders and inhabitants of Harlem for their creatures feeding and going to salt. . . . In witness whereof we the said arbitrators have hereunto set our hands and seals, the thirtieth day of May, in the twenty sixth year of the reign of our sovereign lord King George the Second, Anno. Dom. one thousand seven hundred and fifty three. Abm. Van Wyck ⊕ Abrahm. Lefferts ⊕ Lewis Morris. ⊕

Sealed and delivered
by Messrs. Abr. Van Wyck
and Abr. Leffert
In the presence of us
   Peter Clopper,
   Andw. Breasted.

Sealed and delivered
by Lewis Morris, Esq.
In the presence of us
   Ts. Shepherd,
   Elizabeth Leggett.

    The foregoing taken by me from a very old copy indorsed "A True Copy taken from the original Septr. 1st 1766, by me John Bogert, Junr."
                               James Riker.

I conclude that Benson paid the £160, and received his deed and for three reasons:

1st. He had previously negotiated for the purchase of the Mill Camp, and had *given bonds* to stand by the award.

2nd. A receipt from the elders and deacons for £248; 12: 6, as proceeds of "the sold land", (£248 being just the amount due from Benson and others to whom land was awarded), dated Aug. 30, 1753, three months to a day from the date of the award, shows that the moneys were actually paid in.

3d. Benson remained in undisturbed possession of the Mill Camp. J. R.

Certificate of James Riker, Esq., author of the History of Harlem, authenticating Dutch documents.

To
   John W. Pirsson, Esq.
      Counsellor at Law,
         New York.

Dear Sir,

    I do certify that I have access to the original Records of the town of "New Harlem", now extant; that I am sufficiently conversant with the ancient Dutch text to read and translate it; that the documents and instruments contained in the foregoing paper marked Appendix B. are translations made by me from the originals, and I verily believe the same to be correct and reliable. The following is a list of the said documents.

1. Agreement for the sale by Jan Lamontagne to Jan Louwe Van Schoonderwoert (Bogert) for sale of Montagne's Point and meadows, dated 18th May 1671.
2. Deed of grant and confirmation of the magistrates of Harlem to John de La Montagne of Montagne's Point and the meadows in the Bay of Hellgate, dated 8 Feby. 1672.

3. Resolution of the Constable and Magistrates, estimate land of Jan Lourens Van Schoonerwoert (Bogert) at 18 morgens, dated Jany 16th. 167 ƒ.
4. Deed by Maria Vermilje, widow of Montagne to Cornelia Everts (wife of Bogert) for the Hop Garden, dated 4th Nov. 1679.
5. Judgment in suit of Joost Van Oblinus vs Jan Louwe (Bogert) in Harlem Court relative to a small meadow in the Bay of Hellgate, Dec. 4. 1679.
6. Deed of the Town of Harlem to Jan Louwe Bogert of Lot No. 25 of the Common lands, dated 21st March 1701.
7. Deed of the Town of Harlem to Jan de Lamaeter for lot No. 26 of the Common lands, 21st March 1701.
8. Minutes of the Town of Harlem relative to building the dam for Delavall's Mill at Harlem Creek, dated Jany 3. 1667.
9. Deed from Mrs. Maria Vermilje, the widow of John Montagne, to John Louwe Bogert, for Montagne's Point and meadows in the Bay of Hell-Gate.
11. Minutes of the Town of Harlem containing grant to Samson Benson to build dam, and Mill on the Mill Camp (in place of the Delavall Mill, gone to decay) dated 23d Oct. 1738.
12. Award of Lewis Morris and others, arbitrators and the concurrence of the Freeholders &c of the Mill Camp property to Benjamin Benson, dated May 30th 1753 (being extracted from "A True copy taken from the original Sept. 1st. 1766, by me John Bogert, Jr.")

Dated Waverly, Tioga County, N. Y. May 14th. 1888.

James Riker.

Waverly,
Tioga County, } ss:
New York.

On the 15th day of May 1888, before me came James Riker to me known to be the same person who subscribed the above certificate and acknowledged to me that he made and signed the same.

W. H. Spaulding,
Justice of the Peace.

State of New York, } ss: I, John J. Van Kleeck
Tioga County Clerk's Office   Clerk of said County
and also Clerk of the County and Supreme Courts held therein, (Courts of Record) do hereby certify that W. H. Spaulding whose name is subscribed to the certificate of proof or acknowledgment of the annexed instrument was, at the date of such certificate, a Justice of the Peace in and for said County, commissioned and Sworn and duly authorized to take the same that I am well acquainted with his hand writing and verily believe that the signature to said certificate is genuine, and that said instrument is executed and acknowledged according to the laws of the State of New York.

In Witness Whereof I have hereunto subscribed my name and affixed the seal of said Courts and County at Owego, this 16 day of May 1888.

L. S.

J. J. Van Kleeck, Clerk.

APPENDIX C, No. 1.

Richard Nicholls' Patent of May, 1666.

A patent granted unto the freeholders and inhabitants of Harlem, alias Lancaster, upon the island of Manhattan, Richard Nicholls, Esquire, Govenor, under his Royal Highness, James Duke of York, &c., of all his territory in America, To all to whom these presents shall come, sendeth greeting. Whereas, there is a certain town or village, commonly called and known by the name of New Harlem, situate and being on the east part of this island, now in the tenure or occupation of several freeholders and inhabitants, who have been at considerable charge in building, as well as manuring, planting and fencing the said towne and lands thereunto belonging. Now for a confirmation unto said freeholders and inhabitants in their enjoyment and possession of their particular lots and estates in the said town, as also for an encouragement to them in their farther improvement of the said land. Know ye, that by virtue of the commission and authority unto me given by his Royal Highness, the Duke of York, I have thought fit to ratify, confirm and grant, and by these presents do ratify, confirm and grant unto the said freeholders and inhabitants, their heirs, successors and assigns, and to each and every of them, their particular lots and estates in the said town or any part thereof. And I do likewise confirm and grant unto the freeholders and inhabitants in general, their heirs, successors and assigns, the privileges of a town, but immediately depending on this city, as being the liberties thereof, moreover, for the better ascertaining of the limits of the lands to the said town belonging: the extent of their bounds shall be as follows, viz:—That from the west side of the fence of the said township, a line be run due west four hundred English poles, without variation of the compass, at the end whereof another line being drawn to run north and south, with the variation, that is to say, north to the very end of a certain piece of meadow ground, commonly called the round Meadow, near or adjoining to Hudson River, and South to the saw mills, over against Hogg Island, commonly called Ferkin's Island it shall be the west bounds of their lands, and all the lands lying and being within the said line so drawn north and south as aforesaid, eastward to the town and Harlem river, as also to the north and east rivers shall belong to the town, together with all the soils, creeks, quarries, woods, meadows, pastures, marshes, waters, fishings, huntings and fowling, and all other profits, commodities, emoluments and hereditaments to the said lands and

premises within the said line belonging, or in any wise
appertaining, with their and every of their appurtenances:—
To have and to hold all and singular the said lands, hereditaments and premises, with their and every of their appurtenances, and of every part and parcel thereof, to the said
freeholders and inhabitants, their heirs, successors and
assigns to the proper use and behoof of the said freeholders
and inhabitants, their heirs, successors and assigns forever.
It is likewise further confirmed and granted, that the inhabitants of said town shall have liberty for the conveniency
of more range of their horses and cattle, to go farther west
into the woods, beyond the aforesaid bounds, as they shall
have occasion, the lands lying within being intended for
ploughing, home pastures, and meadows grounds only.
And no person shall be permitted to build any manner of
house or houses within two miles of the aforesaid limits or
bounds of the said town, without the consent of the inhabitants thereof. And the freeholders and inhabitants of the
said town are to observe and keep the terms and conditions
hereafter expressed, that is to say:—That from and after
the date of these presents, that said town shall no longer
be called New Harlem, but shall be known and called by
the name of Lancaster. And in all deeds, bargains and
sales, records or writings, shall be so deemed, observed and
written; moreover, the said town lying very commodious
for a ferry to and from the main, which may redound to
their particular benefit, as well as to the general good, the
freeholders and inhabitants shall be obliged at their charge,
to build or provide one or more boats for that purpose, fit
for the transportation of men, horses and cattle, for which
there will be such a certain allowance given, as shall be
adjudged reasonable. And the freeholders and inhabitants,
their heirs, successors and assigns are likewise to render
and pay all such acknowledgments and duties as already
are or hereafter shall be constituted and ordained by his
Royal Highness, the Duke of York and his heirs, or such
Governor or Governors as shall from time to time be
appointed and set over them. Given under my hand and
seal, at Fort James, in New York, on Manhattan Island,

the   day of May, in the eighteenth year of the reign
of our sovereign, Lord Charles the Second, by the grace of
God, King of England, Scotland, France and Ireland,
defender of the faith, &c., and in the year of our Lord God,
1666.
                                     Richard Nicholls.

State of New York,
Secretary's Office.

I certify the preceding to be a true copy of certain letters
patent or grant, as of record in this office, in Liber part 1,
page 57 &c.
                       Archibald Campbell,
                                Deputy Secretary.
Albany, October 4, 1816.

APPENDIX C, No. 2.

Richard Nicholls' Patent of 11th October, 1667.

Richard Nicolls, Esq., Governor-General under his Royal
Highness Duke of York and Albany, &c., of all his territories in America, to all to whom these Presents shall come,
sendeth Greeting: Whereas, there is a certain town or village upon this island, Manhattan's, commonly called and
known by the name of New Harlem, situate, lying and being
on the east part of the island, now in the tenure or occupation of several of the freeholders and inhabitants, who
being seated there by authority, have improved a considerable proportion of the lands thereunto belonging, and also
settled a competent number of families thereupon, capable
to make a township. Now for confirmation to the said
freeholders and inhabitants in their possession and enjoyment of the premises, as also for an encouragement to them
in their further improvement of the said lands, Know Ye :
That by virtue of the commission and authority unto me

given by his Royal Highness, I have given, ratified, confirmed and granted by these presents due, give, ratify, confirm and grant unto Thomas Delavall, Esq., John Verveelen, Daniel Tourneur, Joost Oblinus, and Resolved Waldron, as patentees, for and in behalf of themselves and their associates, the freeholders and inhabitants of the said town, their heirs, successors and assigns, All that tract, together with the several parcels of land, which already have or hereafter shall be purchased or procured for and on the behalf of the said town within the bounds and limits hereafter set forth and expressed, viz.: That is to say, from the west side of the fence of the said town, a line being run due west four hundred English poles, without variation of the compass, and at the end thereof, another line being drawn across the island north and south, with the variation, that is to say, north from the end of a certain piece of meadow ground, commonly called the Round Meadow, near or adjoining unto Hudson's or North River, and south to ye place where formerly stood the saw mills, over against Verchens or Hogg Island, in the Sound or East River, shall be the western bounds of their lands, and all the lands lying and being within the said line, to draw north and south as aforesaid, eastward to the end of the town and Harlem River, or any part of the said river on which this island doth abut, and likewise on the North and East Rivers, within the limits aforementioned described, doth and shall belong to the said town; as also four lots of meadow ground upon the Maine, marked with Number 1, 2, 3, 4, lying over against the spring, where a passage hath been used to ford over from this island to the maine, and from thence hither, with a small island, commonly called Stoney Island, lying to the east of the town and Harlem River, going through Bronckx Kill by the little and great Barne's Islands, upon which there are also four other lots of meadow ground, marked with No. 1, 2, 3, 4, together with all the soils, creeks, quarries, woods, meadows, pastures, marshes, waters, lakes, fishing, hawking, hunting and fowling and all other profits, commodities, emoluments and hereditaments, to ye said lands and premises within the said bounds and limits set forth, belonging or in anywise appertaining, and also freedom of commonage of range and feed of cattle and horses, further west into the woods upon this island as well without as within their bounds and limits: To have and to hold all and singular the said lands, islands, commonage, hereditaments and premises, with their every of their appurtenances and every part or parcel thereof, unto ye said patentees and their associates, their heirs, successors and assigns, to the proper use and behoof of the said patentees and their associates, their heirs, successors and assigns forever. And I do hereby likewise ratify, confirm and grant unto the said patentees and their associates, their heirs, successors and assigns, all the rights and privileges belonging to a town within this government, with this proviso or exception: that in all matters of debt or trespass of or above the value of five pounds, they shall have relation to and dependence upon the courts of this city as the other towns have upon the several Courts of Sessions to which they do belong. Moreover the place of their present habitation shall continue and retain the name of New Harlem, by which name and stile it shall be distinguished and known in all bargains and sale deeds and records. And no person whatsoever shall be suffered or permitted to erect any manner of house or building upon this island, within two miles of the limits and bounds aforementioned, without the consent and approbation of the major part of the inhabitants of the said town. And Whereas the said town lies very commodious for a ferry to pass to and from the Main, which may redound to the particular benefit of the inhabitants as well as to a general good, the freeholders and inhabitants of the said town shall, in consideration of the benefits and privileges herein granted, as also for what advantage they may receive thereby, be enjoyned and obliged at their own proper cost and charge, to build or provide one or more boats fit for the transportation of men, horses and cattle, for which there shall be a certain allowance given by each particular person, as shall be ordered and adjudged fit and reasonable, they the said patentees and their associates, their heirs, successors and assigns. Rendering and paying such duties and acknowledgments as now are or hereafter shall be constituted and established by the laws of this government, under the obedience of his Royal Highness, his heirs and successors. Given under my hand and seal, at fort James, in New York, on the Island Manhattan's, in America, the 11th. day of October in the 19th. Year of his Majesties reign, *Annoq Domini*, 1667.

State of New York,
 Secretary's Office.

I have compared the preceding with certain letters patent, as of record in this office, in book of patents No. 4, page 57, &c., and do certify that the same is a correct transcript therefrom, and of the whole of said patent.

Archibald Campbell,
Deputy Secretary.

Albany, February 26, 1836.

APPENDIX C, No. 3.

Dongan Patent of March 1686.

Thomas Dongan, Captain General, Governor in Chief, and Vice Admiral in and over the province of New York and its dependencies thereon, in America, under his Majesty James the Second, by the Grace of God of England, Scotland, France and Ireland, King, defender of the faith &c. to all whom these presents shall come, sendeth greeting :—Whereas, Richard Nicolls Esq. formerly Governor of this province hath by his certain writing or patent, bearing date the eleventh day of October, Anno Dom. one thousand six hundred and sixty seven, did give, ratify, confirm and grant unto Thomas Delavall Esq., John Verveelen, Daniel Tourneur, Joost Oblinus and Resolved Waldron, as patentees, for and on the behalf of themselves and their associates, the freeholders and inhabitants of New Harlem their heirs, successors and assigns, all that tract, together with the several parcels of land, which they then had, or after should be purchased or procured for and on the behalf of the said town, within the bounds and limits hereafter set forth and expressed, viz: that is to say,—From the west side of the fence of the said town, a line being run due west four hundred English poles, without variation of the compass, and at the end thereof another line being drawn cross the island north and south with the variation, that is to say, north from the end of a certain piece of meadow ground, commonly called the Meadow Ground, the round meadow near or adjoining unto Hudson's or the North River, and south to the place where formerly stood the saw mills, over against Verkins or Hogg Island, in the Sound or East River, shall be the western bounds of their lands, and all the lands lying and being within the said line so drawn north and south as aforesaid, eastward to the end of the town and Harlem River, or any part of the said River on which this island doth abut, and likewise on the north and east rivers, within the limits aforementioned described, doth and shall belong to the said town, as also four lots of meadow ground upon the Main marked with number 1, 2, 3, 4 lying over against the spring, where a passage hath been used to ford over from this island to the Main, and from thence hither, with a small island commonly called Stony Island, lying to the east of the town and Harlem River, going through Bronck's Kill, by the little and great Barn's Island, upon which there are also four other lots of meadow ground, marked with number 1, 2, 3, 4, together with all the soils, creeks, quarries, woods, meadows, pastures, marshes, waters, lakes, fishing, hawking, hunting, and fowling, and all other profits, commodities, emoluments and hereditaments to the said land and premises, within the bounds and limits set forth, belonging or in anywise appurtaining, and also freedom of commonage for range and feed of cattle and horses, further west into the woods upon this island, as well without as within their bounds and limits set forth and expressed, to have to hold

all and singular the said lands, island commonage hereditaments and premises, with their and every of their appurtenances, and of every part and parcel thereof, unto the said
patentees and their associates, their heirs, successors and
assigns, to the proper use and behoof of the said patentees
and their associates, their heirs, successors and assigns forever. And whereas, Richard Nicoll, Esq. did likewise
ratify, confirm and grant unto the said patentees and their
associates, their heirs, successors and assigns, all the rights
and privileges, belonging to a town, within this government,
with this proviso or exception, that in all matters of debt
or trespass, of or above the value of five pounds, they shall
have relation unto and dependence upon the Courts of this
City, as the other town have upon the several Courts of
Session to which they do belong, and that the place of their
present habitation shall continue and retain the name of
New Harlem, by which name and style it shall be distinguished and known in all bargains and sales, deeds, writings and records, and that no person whatsoever should be
suffered or permitted to erect any manner of house or
building upon this said island within two miles of the limits
and bounds aforementioned without the consent and approbation of the major part of the inhabitants of the said town,
and whereas the said town lies very commodious for a ferry
to and from the main, which may redound to the particular
benefit of the inhabitants, as well as to a general good, the
freeholders and inhabitants of the said town should, in consideration of the benefits and privileges therein granted, as
also for what advantage they might receive thereby be
enjoyned and obliged at their own proper cost and charge
to build and provide one or more boats fit for the transportation of men, horses or cattle, for which was to be a certain
allowance given by each particular person, as should be
then ordered and adjudged fit and reasonable, they, the
said patentees and their associates, their heirs, successors
and assigns rendering and paying such duties and acknowledgments as then were or after should be established by
the laws of this government, under the obedience of his
Royal Highness, his heirs and successors, as and by the

said patent remaining upon record in the Secretary's Office reference being thereunto had doth fully and at large appear. And whereas the present inhabitants and freeholders of the town of New Harlem aforesaid, have made their application unto me for a full and ample confirmation of their premises to them, their heirs successors and assigns forever, in their quiet and peaceable possession. Now know ye, that by virtue of the commission and authority to me derived and power in me residing in consideration of the premises and of the quit rent hereinafter reserved, I have given, granted, ratified and confirmed, and by these presents do give, grant, ratify and confirm unto Jan Delavall, Resolved Waldron, Joost Van Oblinus, Daniel Tourneur, Adolph Meyer, John Spragge, Jan Hendricks Brevoort, Jan Delamater, Isaac Delamater, Barent Waldron, Johannes Vermelje, Lawrence Jansen, Peter Van Oblinus, Jan Dyckman, Jan Nagle, Arent Harmanse, Cornelis Jansen, Jackeline Tourneur, Hester Delamater, Johannes Verveelen, William Waldron, Abraham Montanie, Peter Parmentier, as patentees, for and on the behalf of themselves the present freeholders and inhabitants of the said town of New Harlem, their heirs, successors and assigns, all and singular the before recited tract, parcel and parcels of land and meadow, butted and bounded as in the said patent is mentioned and expressed together with all and singular the messuages, tenaments, houses, buildings, barns, stables, orchards, gardens, pastures, mills, milldams, runs, streams, ponds, woods, underwoods, trees, timber, fencing, fishing, hawking, hunting and fowling, liberties, privileges, hereditaments and improvements whatsoever to the said tract of land and premises belonging or in anywise appurtaining or accepted, reputed, taken or known or used, occupied and enjoyed, as part, parcel or member thereof, with their and every of their appurtenances, always provided that nothing contained therein shall be construed to prejudice the right of the City of New York, or any other particular right and saving to the said City of New York, and their successors forever, and also saving to every particular person, his heirs and assigns that have any right, interest or estate within the limits of the said town of New Harlem, as well as without the limits of the said town of Harlem, full power, liberty and privilege to build, cultivate and improve all such tracts and parcels of land as the said City of New York now have, or hereafter shall have within or without and adjacent to the limits of the town of Harlem aforesaid, and also the commonage of the town of Harlem above aforesaid, is to be confirmed within the limits aforesaid, and the right of commonage to extend no further, any grant or thing contained herein to the contrary in any wise notwithstanding, to have and to hold the said several tracts and parcels of land and premises, with their and every of their appurtenances, unto them the said John Delavall, Resolved Waldron, Joost Van Oblinus, Daniel Tourneur, Adolph Meyer, John Spragge, Jan Hendrick Brevoort, Jan Delamater, Isaac Delamater, Barent Waldron, Johannes Vermelje, Lawrence Jansen, Jan Dyckman, Jan Nagle, Arent Harmanse, Cornelis Jansen, Peter Van Oblinus, Jacqueline Tourneur, Hester Delamater, Joannes Verveelen, William Waldron, Abraham Montanie, Peter Parmentier, as Patentees for and on the behalf of themselves, their heirs, successors and assigns, to the sole and only proper use, benefit and behoof of the said patentees, their heirs, successors and assigns forever, to be holden of his most sacred Majesty, his heirs and successors in free and common soccage, according to the tenure of East Greenwich, in the county of Kent, in his Majesty's kingdom of England, yielding, rending and paying yearly and every year forever, on or before the five and twentieth day of March in lieu of all services and demands whatsoever, as a quit rent to his most sacred Majesty aforesaid, his heirs and successors, or to such officer or officers as shall be appointed to receive the same, sixteen bushels of good winter merchantable wheat, at the City of New York. In testimony whereof, I have caused these presents to be entered upon record in the Secretary's office, and the seal of the province affixed, this seventh day of March, 1686, and in the third year of his Majesty's reign.

              Tho. Dongan.

May it please your Excellency.
The Attorney General hath perused this Patent, and finds nothing contained therein prejudicial to his masters interest.
Examined, 23rd. March 1686. Ja. Graham.
State of New York,
Secretary's Office.
I have compared the preceding with certain letters patent as of record, in this office, in book of patents, No. 6, page 192 &c. and do certify that the same is a correct transcript therefrom, and of the whole of said patent.
Albany, Feb. 23, 1836. Arch'd Campbell,
Dep. Secretary.
The foregoing patents are contained in "Title to Harlem Commons and Louvre, Abstracts". The spelling of the names of the patentees in some instances are corrected so as to correspond·to those given in Riker's History of Harlem.

APPENDIX D.

Opinion of Richard O'Gorman, Esq., Counsel to the Corporation of New York.

LAW DEPARTMENT,
Office of the Counsel to the Corporation,
NEW YORK, August 1st, 1870.

Hon. RICH'D B. CONNOLLY, Comptroller, &c.:

DEAR SIR:—

I have the honor to acknowledge the receipt of your communication, in which you request my opinion whether certain lands in the Harlem River between 91st and 104th Streets, and 107th and 108th Streets, extending to the 3d Avenue, are owned by the city under the provisions of any of the charters and grants vesting the city with the title to land under water.

In answer thereto I beg leave to say:

A claim on behalf of the city to the lands in question can only be urged under the 3d section of the Dongan Charter of 22d of April, 1686, which grants to the Corporation of the City of New York all the waste, vacant, unpatented and unappropriated lands lying and being within the City of New York and on Manhattan Island, extending and reaching to the low water mark, &c., not theretofore given or granted by any of the former Governors or Lieutenants or Commanders-in-Chief, or by any of the former Mayors or Deputy Mayors, or Aldermen of the said city.

I am of the opinion that this grant did not convey the land in question for the following reasons, viz.:

1st. In May, 1666, Governor Nicoll granted and conveyed to "the Inhabitants and Freeholders of Harlem," their successors and assigns forever, a large tract of land (embracing the land in question) by the following descripiont: "All the land in Manhattan Island lying eastward and northward of a line commencing on the East River at the saw mills over against Hogges or Vercher's Island, and running due north until it strikes the Hudson River at the round meadows, together with all soils, meadows, creeks, marshes, waters, fishing, &c.

"Hogges Island is now called Blackwell's Island."

Hoffman's Title of Corporations, Vol. 1, page 147.

Another patent was made to the said Inhabitants, &c., of Harlem, on the 11th of October, 1666, granting the same privileges and the same lands as were embraced in the former patent (of May), but reserving payment of certain duties, which did not, however, impair the force of the granting words of the patent.

On the 7th of March, 1686, Governor Dongan confirmed these patents or grants to the said inhabitants, &c., of Harlem.

See Book of Patents No. 6, page 192, in office of Sec'y of State.

The boundaries and division line between the common lands of the then town of Harlem and the then City of New York were definitely settled under the colonial Act of 1774.

Laws of 1774, 1775, pages 171, 172 and 173.
Also Valentine's Laws, page 1156.

The division line began on the East River, about 74th Street, crossed 2d Avenue at 79th Street, and struck the Hudson River about 129th Street.

2d. The lands in question are marsh or meadow lands lying along the Harlem River, above the original high water line, and not between the lines of high and low water.

They are designated as marshes or meadow land on the old maps of the city.

Vide Commissioner's Map, 1807.
Blue Book Maps.
Dripp's Map of the City of New York, 1867, compiled from surveys of Randall and Blackwell.

The grants to the said " Inhabitants, &c., of Harlem," in express terms, included all marshes, meadows, creeks and soils, and in my opinion embraced all lands, whether marsh or meadow lands, to the ordinary line of high water of the East or Harlem Rivers, although the same were sometimes, and at unusually high tides, partially or wholly submerged.

Rogers v. *Jones*, 1 Wendell, 237.

The terms "Marshes and Meadows" used in the Nicolls charter of 1666, seems to me to be an apt and proper designation of land situate as are the lands in question.

These lands were claimed by the said inhabitants, &c., of Harlem, under the grants and patents above mentioned, and were conveyed by them in the year 1672.

The competency of the inhabitants and freeholders of Harlem to take, hold and convey land was recognized and approved by the Colonial Legislature in the enactment of the Laws of 1774 above referred to, appointing Commis sioners to define the boundaries thereof, and subsequently by the Act of 1820, whereby the State Legislature provided that the land acquired by and under the patents and grants above mentioned, and not previously conveyed by them, shall be sold for the benefit of the inhabitants, &c., of Harlem.

Chapter 115, Laws of 1820.

I am unable to discover in the various charters of the city or in any of the grants of lands under water to the corporation, any provisions which vest in the Mayor, &c., of the City of New York, any title to the land in question.

Yours truly,
RICHARD O'GORMAN,
Counsel to the Corporation.

APPENDIX E.

Opinion of William C. Whitney, Esq., Counsel to the Corporation of New York.

LAW DEPARTMENT,
Office of the Counsel to the Corporation,
NEW YORK, November 10, 1880.

Hon. JOHN KELLY, Comptroller, etc.:

SIR:—I have received your letter of November 4th transmitting the application made to the Commissioners of the Sinking Fund, by William F. Russell, Receiver of the Sixpenny Savings Bank, for a release of whatever claim, if any, the City of New York may possess to certain lands, formerly under water, in certain streams, subject to the flow of tide water, running through the block bounded by 101st and 102d Streets and the 2d and 3d Avenues, which streams have been filled up by the improvements made on the said premises, leaving no vestige thereof.

You then ask my advice as to the rights of the City in this land, and what action, if any, may legally be taken by the Commissioners of the Sinking Fund to grant the relief asked for in said application.

I am aware of only one source from which it may be supposed that title to the lands in question has been derived by the Mayor, Aldermen and Commonalty of the City of New York, namely, the Dongan Charter, granted the 27th of April, 1686, by which the Sovereign "gave and granted unto the Mayor, Aldermen and Commonalty of the City of New York, all the waste, vacant, unpatented and unappropriated lands lying and being within the said City of New York, and of Manhattan Island aforesaid, extending and reaching to the low water mark in, by and through all parts of the said City of New York and Manhattan Island aforesaid, with all the rivers, rivulets, coves, creeks, ponds, waters and water-courses, in the said City and Island, or either of them, not heretofore given and granted by any of the former governors, lieutenants, or commanders-in-chief, under their, or some of their hands and seals, or seal of the Province, or by any of the former Mayors or Deputy Mayors and Aldermen of the said City of New York, to some respective person or persons, late inhabitants of the said City of New York or Manhattan Island, or of other parts of the said province."

The grant thus made was subsequently confirmed by the Montgomerie Charter, January 15th, 1730, and is sufficiently broad to include the lands in question if such lands had not theretofore been granted by competent authority.

Such a prior grant is found in the patent, dated May, 1666, granted by Richard Nicolls, Governor, unto the freeholders and inhabitants of Harlem.

In said grant it is provided that the extent "of their bounds shall be as follows, viz.: That from the west side of the fence of the said township a line be run due west four hundred English poles without variation of the compass, at the end whereof another line being drawn to run north and south with the variation, that is to say, north to the end of a certain piece of meadow ground commonly called the Round Meadow, near or adjoining the Hudson River, and south to the sawmills over against Hogg Island, commonly called Forkins Island, it shall be the west bounds of their lands, and all the lands lying and being within the said line so drawn north and south, as aforesaid, eastward to the town and Harlem River, as also to the North and East Rivers, shall belong to the town, together with all the soils, creeks, quarries, woods, meadows, pastures, marshes, waters, fishings, huntings and fowling, and all other profits, commodities, emoluments and hereditaments to the said lands and premises within the said line belonging, or in anywise appertaining, with their, and every of their, appurtenances, to have and to hold all and singular the said lands, hereditaments and premises within their, and every of their, appurtenances and every part and parcel thereof, to the said freeholders and inhabitants, their heirs, successors and assigns, to the proper use and behoof of the said freeholders and inhabitants, their heirs, successors and assigns forever."

Vide Liber No. 1, page 57, Record of Patents, Office of the Secretary of State.

The above-mentioned patent was confirmed by a further patent, granted by Governor Nicolls, October 11, 1666.

Vide Book of Patents No. 4, page 57.

The patent was further confirmed by grant made by Thomas Dongan, Captain-General, etc., dated March 7, 1686, recorded in Book of Patents No. 6, page 192.

The last-named patent confirmed to the "freeholders and inhabitants of the said town of New Harlem, their heirs, successors and assigns, all and singular the before-recited tract, parcel and parcels of land and meadow, butted and bounded as in the said patent is mentioned and expressed, together with all and singular the messuages, tenements, houses, buildings, barns, stables, orchards, gardens, pastures, mills, mill-dams, runs, streams, ponds, woods, underwoods, trees, timber, fencing, fishing, hawking, hunting and fowling, liberties, privileges, hereditaments and improvements whatsoever to the said tract of land and premises belonging or in anywise appertaining or accepted, reputed, taken or known or used, occupied and enjoyed as part or member thereof, with their and every of their appurtenances."

It is, therefore, plain that the lands and appurtenances granted to the freeholders and inhabitants of Harlem were saved and excepted from the operation of the grant made by Governor Dongan to the Mayor, Aldermen and Commonalty of the City of New York on the 27th day of April, 1686.

Subsequently to these grants controversies arose between the freeholders and inhabitants of Harlem and the City of New York in relation to the boundaries of the land acquired by each, under their respective grants.

In order to settle and determine such controversies, an Act was procured to be passed on the 24th day of March, 1772, by which Commissioners were named to fix upon and settle, and ascertain the boundaries, between the township of Harlem and the lands granted to the Mayor, Aldermen and Commonalty of the City of New York.

The proceedings of the Commissioners under such Act were confirmed by an Act passed April 3, 1775.

Vide Laws of New York, 1774 and 1775, pp. 171 and 172.

It is understood that Hogg Island, named in the grant, is now called Blackwell's Island.

Vide Hoffman's Estate and Rights of the Corporation, Vol. I., p. 147.

The report of the Commissioners is recorded in the Register's office in the City of New York, wherein the extent and boundaries of Harlem Commons is set out by them.

The division line began on the East River, about 74th Street, crossed 2d Avenue at or near 79th Street, and struck the Hudson River at about 129th Street.

It seems, therefore, that the premises in question are included within the grant to the freeholders and inhabitants of Harlem, and that the Mayor, Aldermen and Commonalty of the City of New York have acquired no title thereto under their charters.

The title of the freeholders and inhabitants of Harlem to the common lands acquired under the above-recited grants, was transferred, by Act of the Legislature passed March 28, 1820, to trustees therein named and declared to be trustees in behalf of the said freeholders and inhabitants of Harlem, and seized in fee simple of the common lands, in trust, however, for the said freeholders and inhabitants, and invested with power to take possession of the said common lands, etc.

The Act further confers power upon the said trustees to sell the lands, and makes direction as to the disposition of the proceeds of such sale.

The validity of the last-recited Act has been passed upon by Chancellor Kent, in an opinion given by him August 23, 1825, in relation to the title of a purchaser from said trustees.

I am, therefore, of the opinion, and advise you, that the Mayor, Aldermen and Commonalty of the City of New York have no right in the lands in question, and therefore, no action in relation thereto, by the Commissioners of the Sinking Fund, would be legal or proper.

Yours respectfully,
(sgd) WILLIAM C. WHITNEY,
Counsel to the Corporation.

APPENDIX F.

Opinion of the Hon. Murray Hoffman relating to Harlem Mill Creek.

Mr. Voorhis is the owner of a piece of ground, lying between the Second and Third Avenues, on the northerly side of 108th Street stretching toward 109th Street. I shall assume for this opinion, that at the time of the Patents,

Deeds and Statutes hereafter mentioned, down to 1775, a portion of the ground in question lay between high and low water mark, affected by the flux and reflux of the tide coming from an arm of the sea. But when the locality is fully understood, this proposition may admit of doubt. The exact position of the parcel must be more definitely pointed out.

The general course of Harlem River from Benson's Point near 106th Street to about 117th Street is northerly. About 107th Street a body of water sets up from the river which I call Harlem River. It is sometimes marked as the East River. It stretches from the river westerly and was known as Harlem Creek, sometimes Montanya's Creek.

About midway between 107th and 108th Streets a cove sets up northwardly from the general course of this creek and extends toward 109th Street. At the extremity of this cove is the strip of land in question covered at high water.

On the northern line of 108th Street, and between Second and Third Avenues, was a mill, a mill pond toward Third Avenue, and the water leaving the mill ran into this cove. There was a mill-dam just beyond Third Avenue.

This mill had been projected in 1661, when the Montanya's family petitioned the authorities of Harlem for certain privileges for families about to settle near the site. It was erected before 1747, but when I have not traced. It is stated that small vessels or barges could come up to the mill at ordinary high water.

In the year 1837, the Second Avenue was opened according to law, and in the year 1849 was graded and traveled. Culverts were made at various points, but it is plain that there was no longer any flux or re-flux of the tide at the place in question, and navigability of any description was destroyed to westward of Second Avenue.

I proceed to state the patents, &c., bearing upon the question, on the fact as assumed. The Patent of Governor Nicolls, of May, 1666, was entitled "A Patent granted to the Inhabitants and Freeholders of Harlem, alias Lancaster, upon the Island of Manhattan." It contained a grant as follows: I likewise grant unto the freeholders and inhabitants in general, their successors and assigns, the privileges of a town. The extent of their bounds shall be as follows, viz.: From the west side of the fence of the said township, a line be run due west four hundred English poles, without variation of the compass, at the end whereof another line being drawn to north and south with the variation, that is to say, north to the very end of a certain piece of meadow ground, commonly called the Round Meadows, near or adjoining to Hudson River, and south to the saw mills over and against Hogg Island, commonly called Ferkins Island, it shall be the west bounds of the said land and all the lands lying and being within the said line so drawn north and south as aforesaid, eastward to the town and *Harlaem River and also to the North and East Rivers*, shall belong to the town, together with all the soyles, creeks, quarries, woods, meadows, pastures, marshes, waters, fishing and all other profits, hereditaments, &c.

The confirmation by Nicolls, of October, 1667, varies in these particulars: The island is called Vercher's or Hogg Island, in the Sound or East River, and after the words Harlem River, above italicised, is added: "or any part of the said river on which this island doth abut."

This second patent is to Thomas Delavall and others as patentees for themselves and associates, the freeholders and inhabitants of the town.

The confirmation by Dongan, of the 7th of March, 1687, is also to the patentees, and adds the words: Mills, milldams, runs, streams, ponds, wood, &c. The Round Meadow of the Patent was a lot of salt meadow just north of Manhattanville, near the foot of 129th Street.

It is needless to attempt an explanation of these boundary lines. The settlement under the Act of 1772, ratified in 1775, must be taken as defining them, as matter of fact. But we notice that the rivers named are the Hudson River, the East River and the Harlem River. The Verchen (Blackwell's Island) lies in the East River, and we may conclude what other proofs show, that the East River proper ended at about 89th Street, opposite Middle Reef, and Harlem River was the arm beyond Gracie's Point.

Here it seems was the point of division according to grant and records. We notice also that it is the river to which the grant extends.

On the 10th of March, 1772, a Bill was brought from the Assembly to the Legislative Council entitled "An Act to settle and *establish* the line or lines of a division between the City of New York and the township of Harlem, so far as concerns the right of soil in controversy. On the 12th March it passed the Council, and on the 24th was approved by the Governor. The boundary having been settled, an Act was passed on the 3d of April, 1775, "To confirm the proceedings of the Commissioners heretofore appointed by a law of this colony, to settle the line or lines of division between the City of New York and the township of Harlem, and for establishing the boundary line between said city and township."

The Statute of 1772 provided that the settlement of the line when recorded shall operate as a total extinguishment of all claim, title and interest of the township, and all persons, &c., in and to the lands to the southward and westward of such division line, and shall also operate as a total extinguishment of all the right, title and interest of the City of New York to all lands, &c., which shall lie to the northward and southward of the said division line so to be ascertained and run out, the lands lying and being between high and low water mark within the City of New York to the northward and eastward of the said division line only excepted.

The City of New York, jurisdictionally at any rate, included the lands to low water mark, even on the Westchester side of Harlem River.

The Statutes of 1775 ratified and confirmed the proceedings of the Commissioners, and we understand that the boundaries thus adjusted have remained unaltered and unquestioned since. The line ran by the Commissioners commenced on the East River at 74th Street, crossed the Second Avenue at 79th Street, the Third Avenue at 81st Street and struck the Harlem River near 129th Street.

Another and most important fact is the establishment of

the title to the parcel in question. From the various deeds, abstracts of which are hereto annexed, maps, survey, old records and documents and statements of persons acquainted with the antiquities of Harlem, I am fully satisfied that this parcel was included in the partition which took place in 1711, 1712, among the inhabitants, freeholders and the representatives of the Patentees. It deserves especial notice that Thomas Delavall was one of the Patentees, that each Patentee was to have twelve acres (sixty in all) and that in the deed of 1747, the parcel conveyed to Benson is called Delavall's land. Upon these documents and Statutes I consider, 1st. That the best construction of the Patents and confirmation is that the strip between high and low water (the tideway as it is conveniently called) passed to the freeholders, &c., of Harlem. The grant embraces "lands, soyles, waters, streams, meadows, marshes, runs, creeks and ponds." It would be difficult to get together terms which would more fully embrace anything of land, of water, and of any combination of the two. The word creek is as pertinent to a body of salt water as to one of fresh. In the Statute 5 and 6 Edw., 6th chap. 14, any one bringing any wares, &c., toward any city, port, haven, creek or road of the realm from any port beyond sea should be subject to a penalty as provided. So in the Statue 5 Eliz., chap. 5, § 8, it is forbidden to bring fishing vessels owned by strangers into any port or creek of the realm.

It is defined in the Encyclopedia a port of a haven where anything is landed from the sea. So in Cunningham's Law Dictionary it is a port of a haven where anything is landed from the sea. And in Henry 4, chap. 40, we have : in great ports of the sea, and not in Crykes or small "arrivals." We can here draw a natural, and we think, legal distinction between the River proper and a creek of it. The former is *defined* by the general course (*filum*) of the body of the stream, and such course is from point to point, where there is an indentation into the land, properly a cove. The latter is that indentation. And we could very consistently hold that the land under water, within the cove, between high and low water, passed, but not outside of it.

This view would be tenable even if that was an indentation from Harlem River; *a fortiori* when from Harlem Creek. But the creek itself, we contend, passed, and the case is then much stronger.

Again, we have the words "waters, lands and *soyles*." What is the meaning of this last word? The Lord Chancellor, in the Attorney General *vs*. Johnson (12 Wilson, Rep. 95) says, "A grant includes the water between high and low water mark, if it covers the *soil*." The right of wreck, says Lord Hale, affords a strong presumption that the soil is intended to pass (cited Hoffman's Law of the Corporation, etc., Appendix 108).

So in the important case of Logen *vs*. Jones, 1 Wendell, it is said, "The King has the property *tam aquae quam soli*." So in the Rivers which have the flux and re-flux of the sea. But by grant or prescription the subject may have the interest in the water *and* soil of navigable rivers.

Instances are cited by Lord Hale of words in a grant sufficient to convey this right. But as the river is the boundary, there could be no pretence for carrying it beyond ow water mark. Thus the right of the State is retained to the *navigable* rivers in its true sense, and effect is given to the word *soyle*, which otherwise would convey nothing which is not conveyed by other words. There is, then, legal ground for holding that the slip between high and low water passed by the patents, and particularly at the locality of the property in question.

But the Act of 1772, and the confirmatory Act of 1775, create a difficulty. It is obvious that there was a controversy as to the rights of soyle between Harlem and the Corporation of New York ; and we are to remember that, under the charters of Dongan 1686, and of Montgomery 1730, the corporation became entitled to all waste, vacant and unpatented land on Manhattan Island reaching to low water mark. (See Hoffman's Treatise, vol. 1, p. 180, etc.)

Here then is an express Legislative enactment that the title of New York shall not be extinguished by the Commissioners, adjustment of bounds, in the parcels between high and low water within the City. The City *limits* included all, even to low water on the Westchester side. Then the fact that the parcel in question was comprised in the deeds consequent upon the partition of 1711 is most important. A title became vested in an individual before the statutes of 1772 and 1775. The source of such title was either old Dutch Ground Briefs before 1666, in which case the Patents of Nicolls operated as confirmation, or a direct grant by the proper officers of Harlaem under the patents, (of which there was an example in February 1672) or a confirmatory grant under the Patents of an older title. In Delavall's case the conclusion is next to a certainty, that he took under the Patent whether he had any title before or not. Then his title goes back to 1747, at least, and the action of the Legislature in the Statutes referred to, was wholly inoperative to divest a vested right, interest or title.

Let us concede which admits of strong argument, that it amounts to an express legislative declaration that the title was in the City of New York, not merely that the adjustment should not impair whatever title they had; concede also that it was competent for the authorities of Harlaem to compromise the interests of the town in this *respect:* To restrict any right the town and inhabitants had to the tideway. This could only be for the future. It is impossible that the compromise or surrender could in any form or manner prejudice or affect the right of a grantee acquiring title before the arrangement and getting it under the Patents. The *quasi* corporation might bind for all future grants, but could not take away rights conferred under previous ones.

Thus we are come back to the question whether the several patents covered the soil under water at the place in question. If any conclusion had been that the strip in question could not be considered as having passed under the Patent, then it did pass under the charter to the Corporation of the city giving them the waste, vacant, unpatented lands around the Island to low water mark. This grant and its extent is discussed in Hoffman's Treatise, (Vol. 1, p. 183.) And it is considered that it covers the tideway, even where the upland adjoining was vested in another by a grant before 1686, but not comprising the tideway. But the Corporation in exercise of the power conferred by statutes, a portion of the power of eminent domain delegated to them, have opened the Second Avenue and effectually *destroyed* the navigability of the cove at this place in question, and all the advantages once arising from it.

Now on the assumption that the title was in the Corporation, this was an inquiry to interest or right, to be claimed and paid for, or compensated by benefits. The lands which clearly passed were subject to the exercise of this power of opening avenues and streets for public use; and the benefit arising from the flow of water at the place, and every possible interest in the soil was, of course, as liable. Even the late important case of Gates *v.* The City of Milwaukee is entirely consistent with this view. (See Gerard's Treatise, p. 14). Upon the whole I conclude that the title and right to the strip in question did pass under the patents, was vested before or in the year 1747, in one claiming under the patents could not be affected by the statutes of 1772 and 1775, and is now vested in Mr. Voorhis.

New York, March 13, 1873. (Signed) MURRAY HOFFMAN.

APPENDIX G.

Second Avenue Opening—Extracts from Report of Commissioners.

1836, Sept. 23. Petition filed for appointment of Commissioners, opening from 86th to 109th Street.
1837, Apl. 5. Report and additional Report of Commissioners, opening, 86th to 109th Street.

Extract from Report of Commissioners, in the matter of opening Second Avenue, from 86th to 109th Street in the Twelfth Ward of the City of New York. (R. Emmet, Att'y) "And we, the Commissioners, do further report, that all that certain lot, piece or parcel of land situate, lying and being in the 12th ward of said City and bounded and containing as follows, to wit: Beginning at the southwesterly corner of 107th Street, as established by law and the Second Avenue as the same is to be opened, and running thence southwesterly along the northerly line or side of the Second Avenue as the same is to be opened one hundred feet ten inches, to land of James Chesterman; thence southeasterly along the same fifty feet to a line drawn through the centre of the Second Avenue as the same is to be opened; thence northwesterly along the same fifty feet to the northerly line or side of the Second Avenue as the same is to be opened, and running thence southwesterly along the same thirty feet to the place of beginning, is also required for the purpose of opening the said Avenue as aforesaid.

"And we, the said Commissioners, do further report, that William P. Hallett is seized in fee of, in and to the last described piece or parcel of land.

"And we, the said Commissioners, do further report, that the said William P. Halleck is also seized of, in and to all that certain other lot, piece or parcel of land situate, lying and being northwesterly of and adjoining the last-described piece or parcel of land required for the purpose aforesaid, and bounded and containing as follows, to wit: Beginning at the southwesterly corner of 107th Street, as established by law and the Second Avenue, as the same is to be opened, and running thence southwesterly along the northwesterly line or side of the Second Avenue, as the same is to be opened, one hundred feet and ten inches, to the northeasterly line or side of land of James Chesterman; thence nothwesterly along the same three hundred and five feet to a line drawn at the half distance between the Second Avenue as the same is to be opened and the Third Avenue, as established by law; thence northeasterly along the same one hundred and thirty feet ten inches, to a line drawn through the centre of One Hundred and Seventh Street as established by law; thence southeasterly three hundred and five feet to the northwesterly line or side of the Second Avenue as the same is to be opened, and running thence southwesterly along the same thirty feet to the place of beginning.

"And we, the said Commissioners, do further report, that we have assessed the benefit and advantage to the said William P. Hallett from the said opening of the Second Avenue as aforesaid, by and in consequence or relinquishing his interest in the last-described piece or parcel of land required for the purpose aforesaid over and above the loss and damage to him by reason of his interest in the last-described adjoining piece or parcel of land to amount to the sum of $19.

"And we, the said Commissioners, do further report, that all that certain lot, piece or parcel of land situate, lying and being in the Twelfth Ward of the said city, and bounded and described as follows: Beginning at the northeasterly corner of Second Avenue, as the same is to be opened, and One Hundred and Seventh Street as established by law, and running thence northeasterly along the southeasterly line or side of Second Avenue, as the same is to be opened, about thirty-six feet be the same more or less, to the centre of Harlem Creek; thence northwesterly along the same one hundred feet to the northwesterly line or side of Second Avenue as the same is to be opened; thence southwesterly along the same sixty-six feet be the same more or less, to a line drawn through the centre of 107th Street, as the same is established by law; thence southeasterly along the same one hundred feet to the southeasterly line or side of the Second Avenue as the same is to be opened, and running thence northeasterly along the same thirty feet to the place of beginning, is also required for the purpose of opening Second Avenue, as aforesaid.

"And we, the said Commissioners, do further report, that Charles H. Hall is seized in fee of, in and to the last-described piece or parcel of land.

"And we, the said Commissioners, do further report, that the said Charles H. Hall is also seized in fee of, in and to all that certain other lot, piece or parcel of land situate, lying and being northwesterly of and adjoining the last-described piece or parcel of land, and bounded and containing as follows, to wit: Beginning at the northwesterly corner of the said Second Avenue as the same is to be opened, and 107th Street as established by law, and running thence northeasterly along the northwesterly line or side of the Second Avenue as the same is to be opened, about thirty-six feet be the same more or less, to the centre of Harlem Creek; thence northwesterly along the same three hundred and five feet to a line drawn at the half distance between the Second Avenue as the same is to be opened, and the Third Avenue as established by law, and running thence southwesterly along the said line sixty feet be the same more or less, to a line drawn through the centre of 107th Street as established by law; thence southeasterly along the same three hundred and five feet to the northwesterly line or side of the Second Avenue as the same is to be opened, and running thence northeasterly along the same thirty feet to the place of beginning."

(Then follows another description on 107th Street between First and Second Avenues.)

"And we, the said Commissioners, do further report, that we have estimated and assessed the benefit and advantage to the said Charles H. Hall from the said opening of the Second Avenue as aforesaid, by and in consequence of relinquishing his interest in the last-described piece or parcel of land required for the purpose aforesaid, over and above the loss and damage to him by reason of his interest in the last-described adjoining piece or parcel of land, to amount to the sum of Four dollars."

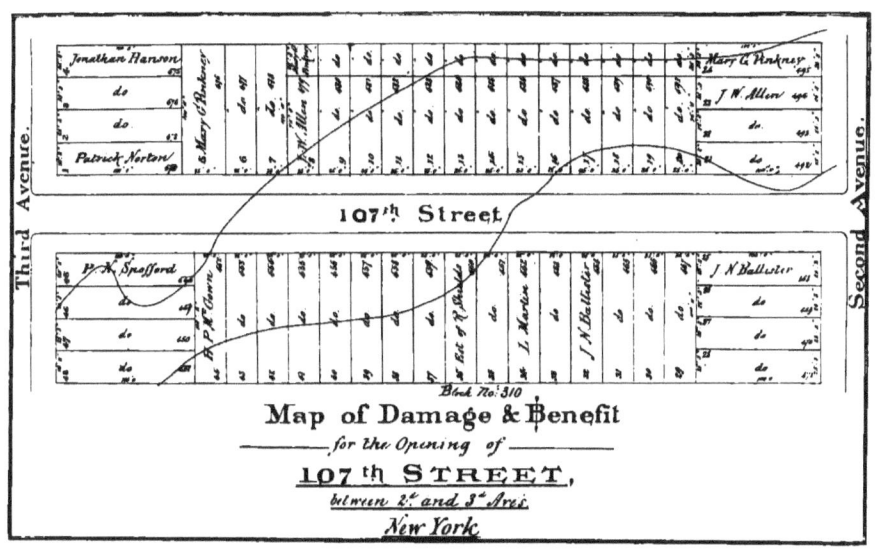

Map of Damage & Benefit
for the Opening of
107th STREET,
between 2d and 3d Aves.
New York

APPENDIX H.

Extract from Proceedings for the Opening of 106th and 107th Streets between the Fifth Avenue and the East River, New York, 1871.

1871, Aug. 2, Petition and order filed appointing Commissioners.
1872, Dec. 11, Report of Commissioners, 1 Vol. Benefit and damage.
1872, Nov. 8, Order confirming Report of Commissioners.

Extract for Assessment List.
Assessment for Benefit.

Commencing on the Southwest corner of 107th Street and Third Avenue.

Ward Block.	No. lot.	Map No.	Owners.	Benefit, Dol. Cts.
310	45	448	P. N. Spofford.	52
"	46	449	"	21
"	47	450	"	13
"	48	451	"	6
"	44	452	H. P. McGown.	25
"	43	453	"	25
"	42	454	"	25
"	41	455	"	25
"	40	456	"	25
"	39	457	"	25
"	38	458	"	25
"	37	459	"	25
"	36	460	Estate of R. Shields.	25
"	35	461	"	25
"	34	462	L. Martin.	25
"	33	463	"	25
"	32	464	J. N. Ballister.	25
"	31	465	"	25
"	30	466	"	25
"	29	467	"	25
"	28	468	"	48
"	27	469	"	18
"	26	470	"	10
"	25	471	"	5

See extract of Map filed with Commissioners' Report.

Appendix I.

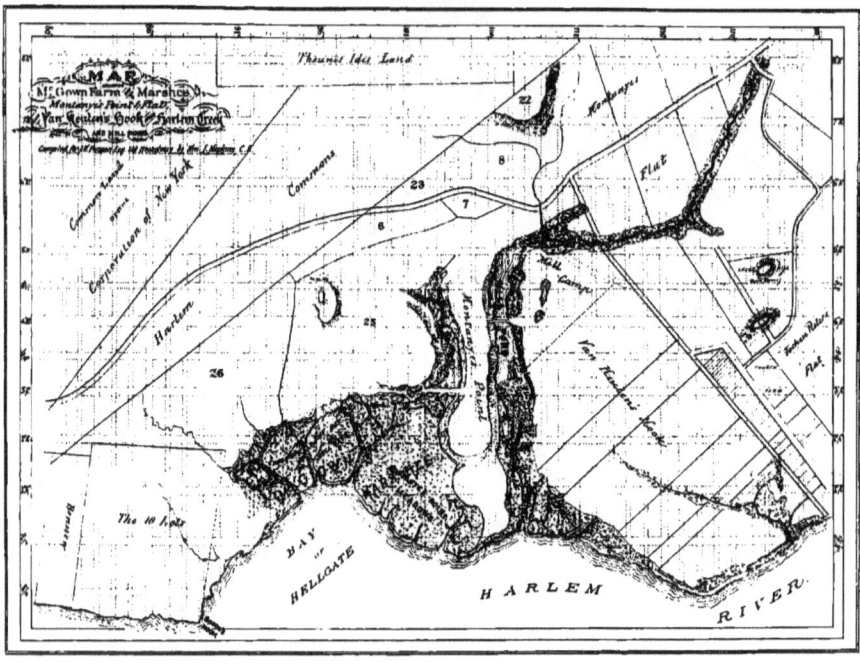

INDEX.

Abbott, *Ch. J.:* Opinion in Vooght *v.* Wynch (2 B. & A.), as to navigable waters... 47
Abstract of Title: To McGown's marshes..............1, 85, 102, 103
    Opinions as to title... 106
    To Harlem Creek and Mill Pond................................ 107
    Opinion as to title... 128
Allen, Senator: Opinion in Canal Commissioners *v.* The People (5 Wend., 452).. 55
    The common law as it existed in 1775 cannot be altered so as to affect grants existing prior to that date..................... 55
American Authorities: On the subject of tidal waters not harmonious.. 57
    Decisions criticising the supposed common law doctrine as to the ebb and flow of the tide considered.....................58, 59
Andros, Governor: Proclamation by, November, 1674............. 4
Archer, John, of Yonkers Land: Claims some of the meadows in Harlem River... 85
Appendix A 130, B 137, C 156, D 167, E 170, F 174, G 181, H 185
Bailey, *J.:* Opinion in Rex *v.* Montague (4 B. & C., 601), ebb and flow of the tide, not the test of a river being navigable...... 46
    In Vooght *v.* Winch (2 B. & A.), obstruction to navigable river, twenty years effect of................................. 47
Barents Islands..14, 86
Bay of Hell Gate... 1
    Description of..85, 86
    Meadows in, classified...................................... ib.
    Title to... ib.
Beardsley, Senator: Opinions of, in *Ex parte* Tibbets (5 Wend., 423)... 59
Benson, Johannes: Grantee of Bogert of Montagne Point farm... 98
Benson, Samson: Son of Johannes, acquires title to Montagne's Point farm... 99
Benson, Samson: Great grandson of Johannes and father of Margaret McGown... 1
Benson, Benjamin: Son of Samson, and grandson of Johannes, acquires title to Montagne's Point farm, also to the Mill Pond and farm on northerly side of Harlem Creek.................. 100
Benson, Peter B.: Son of Benjamin, acquires title to the Mill Pond and farm on the northerly side of Harlem Creek...... 114
    Will of... 118

INDEX.

Benson, Benjamin P. : Son and one of the devisees of Peter B..... 119
Benson, Wilhelmina : Daughter of Benjamin P., and wife of Peter
    Van Arsdale 119
Blackstone, Sr., Wm : Sources of municipal law................... 33
    Navigable rivers 44
    No reference to ebb and flow of tide as a test of a river being
        public... 45
    Variant decisions tested by 67
Blackburn, Ld. : Opinion of, in Bristow v. Cormican (3 App. Cas.,
    641), as to whether the crown has a *prima facie* title to soil
    of a lake... 49
Bracton : As to source of title to sea shore........................... 33
Breen v. Lock (11 N. Y. State Reporter, 288): Compared with
    Roberts v. Baumgarten 63
    Involved title to soil to one of the extinct Harlem creeks and,
    in effect, held that it was not a navigable river.............. 63
British : Claims to New Netherland considered, founded on dis-
    covery and not on conquest..................................... 2
    Occupation by in 1664... ib.
    Condition of Dutch titles at that time........................... ib.
Broadhead : History State N. Y., as to forcible entry of British.... 3
    Reoccupation by Dutch .... ib.
Bronk's Kill 86
Bronson, J. : As to Indian titles.. 9
    Opinion of, in Child v. Starr (20 Wend., 149)................. 59
    The ebb and flow of the tide furnishes an imperfect standard
    for determining what rivers are navigable..................... 59
Campbell, Ld. : Opinion in McCannon v. Sinclair (Ellis & Ellis R.,
    54).. 49
Canal Street Creek... 84
Carteret, James : Deed to, from Thos. Delavall..................... 109
Carteret, Elizabeth : Daughter of James Carteret, married to Philip
    Pipon... 110
Civil Law : Never in force in New York 8
Commons, Harlem : Sale of... 14
Common Law : Applicable to the construction of Dutch grants... 8
    Doctrine of, as to the shares of the sea and marshes 43
    As to navigable waters... 44
Common Lands : Division of, in 1691................................. 92
Commissioners : Appointed to make division of common lands.... 92
Conclusion : Doubts in regard to titles to Harlem meadows and
    creeks wholly groundless... 106
    Title, as derived through the Montagnes, John Louwe Bogert,
    Van Oblinus, De Lamater and Town of Harlem, appears to be
    good and valid... 106
    As to the title of the **McGown marshes**....................... 106
Constitution of 1777 54

INDEX.   189

Construction of Title of Samson Benson, Sr., to the Montagne
  Point farm.. 99
    No break in the chain of title............................. ib.
Conveyances: See Deeds.
Corlear's Hook... 19
Cowen, J.: Opinion in Luce v. Carley (24 Wend., 453)........... 116
    Land marks on banks of river not meant to stand on precise
      water line, but merely used to fix the termini of line... 116
Creeks of Ports.. 39
  Prima facie public streams................................. 41
    A creek capable of becoming a port, but not so in fact, is not
      therefore *prima facie* public........................... 41
    Creeks of the the sea...................................... 42
Curler's Hook, or Van Kenlen's Hook: Account of settlement of.. 20
Davis, J.: Opinion of, in People v. Canal Appraisers (33 N. Y., 461),
      that "navigable rivers" means navigable in fact.......... 63
Deeds: Director-General Kieft to Sieur Johannes La Montagne... 21
    Construed.. 31
  Montagnes: Of Montagne's Point and flats..................... 21
    Town of Harlem to John Montagne, Sr., of Montagne's Point
      and meadows.. 30
    Town of Harlem to John Louwe Bogert, of lot 25 of common
      lands in the Bay of Hell Gate......................91, 92
    Town of Harlem to John De Lamater, of lot 26 of common
      lands in the Bay of Hell Gate............................ 93
    John Lowesen Bogert to Johannes Benson, of Montagne's Point
      and meadows.. 95
    Maria, widow of John De La Montagne, of Montagne's Point
      and meadows.. 96
    Samson Benson (son of Johannes): Heirs of, to Benjamin Ben-
      son, Montagne's Point and meadows........................ 99
    Benjamin Benson to Samson Benson (his son): Montagne's
      Point and meadows.. 101
    Construed.. 103
    Margaret McGown to Samson B. McGown: Part of the mead-
      ows in the Bay of Hell Gate.............................. 103
    Margaret McGown to Edward Sandford: Residue of the
      meadows.. 103
    Thomas Delavall to James Carteret and Frances, his wife:
      Lots 22 and 23 on Van Kenlen's Hook, and the Harlem
      Mill property.. 109
    Simon Johnson to Benjamin Benson: Lots 22 and 23 on Van
      Kenlen's Hook.. 111
    Town of Harlem to Benjamin Benson: Grant of the mill right
      on Harlem Creek and of the land known as Mill Camp 112
      and Appendix B... 3
    Benjamin Benson to Peter B. Benson: Of Mill Pond and farm
      on northerly side of Harlem Creek........................ 114

INDEX.

Benjamin P. Benson with Peter Van Arsdale and Wilhelmina,
his wife: In partition... 119
Peter Van Arsdale and Wilhelmina, his wife, to Benjamin L.
Benson.. 120
Same to same... 120
Benjamin P. Benson and wife to Benjamin L. Benson: Two
deeds.. 121
Benjamin L. Benson to Harriet M. Wiswell: Two deeds........ 122
De Forest, Henry: First settlers in Harlem......................... 17
Sailed from the Trexel 1636...................................... ib.
Allotted 200 acres of land on the north-east end of Island....... ib.
See Harlem Farm
De Jure Maris: See Tidal Creeks.
Doubts as to its being the work of Ld. Hale.................. 34
Its maxim to be carefully weighed............................. 34
Ld Hale died in 1676, De Jure Maris not published until 1787.. 45
Certain rules stated therein not now law...................... 35
Considered in reference to the deeds to the Montagnes........ 37
Responsible for the opinion that the King's title extends to all
tidal waters... 43
That doctrine not taught by other treatises.................. 43
De Jure Portibus: See Tidal Creek................................. 39
De Lamater, John: Buys Van Oblinus' farm on Hoorn's Hook.... 93
Lot No. 26 of common lands, joining the farm, set off to him by
the town in the division of 1691............................. 93
See deed, Appendix B, 7.
Delavall, Thomas: One of the patentees in Nicoll's patent......... 15
Treasurer of the colony and Mayor of the City of New York.. 108
Land bought by him of Moseman................................. 109
Directors General: Declaration concerning the house of Jochem
Peterson Kuyter, destroyed by the Indians..................... 26
Division line: Between the farms of Montagne or Bogert and Van
Oblinus... 91
Dongan, Governor: Patent to the town of Harlem of 1686......... 15
....and Appendix C
Charter of the City of New York considered.................... 15
Denman, Ch. J.: Opinion in Mayor Colchester v. Brooke (7, 2 B,
372, 1845)... 48
Also in Williams v. Wilcox (3 Ad & El, 314, 333), also in Rex v.
Landulph (1 Moody & R, 393) as to navigable rivers.......... ib.
Discoveries: Of Gilbert, Sir Walter Raleigh and Hendrick Hudson 2
British title founded on.. ib.
Duke of York.. 3, 5
Patent to Appendix C, No 3.
Dutch, The: Never had any right to New Netherland.............. 8
Claim to New Netherland stated.................................. 2
Grants to be construed by common law........................... 8
Occupation of Manhattan Island.................................. 9

INDEX. 191

Purchase of Manhattan Island from the Indians.............. ib.
Grants and documents.................................Appendix B
Governors: Authority of.................................... 9
Church in Harlem : The original owner of the southerly half of
   the McGown marshes....................................... 88
All questions arising out of grants from, to be construed by
   laws of England prior to American Revolution 7
Dutch Grants : History of 2
   Construction of... 8
English and American Cases: Compared in juxtaposition......... 64
English possessions in America: Claimed by right of discovery... 2
English Rivers : But few naturally navigable except the Thames
   and Severn, but were made so by Act of Parliament 50
English title to New Netherlands indisputable 8
   Common law in force .... ib.
Ferry : To be established near Harlem......................... 25
Finch, J. : Opinion in Mayor v. Hart (95 N. Y., 450) 7
   Common law of England; the law in New Amsterdam......... 7
First Harlem Farm : History of................................ 17
Fountain, The, in Central Park : The source of one of the three
   fresh water streams which emptied into Harlem Creek....... 107
Freeholders : Of Harlem in 1661............................... 28
   And inhabitants of Harlem a civil corporation 12
Fresh Water : The Collect Pond 22
   Creeks or streams 22, 32, 33, 37, 69, 84
Gould : Law of waters; rights of settlers in territories acquired by
   discovery 7
   As to De Jure Maris...................................... 35
Grants : On tidal waters by government construed.............. 42
   Of real property to be construed by the common law 8
   To the City of New York by the Governor did not include the
   McGown or other Harlem marshes 104
Gray, J.: Opinion in Roberts v. Baumgarten (110 N. Y., 380) 54
Ground Brief : The first to any part of Harlem granted by Dutch
   Government 1
   Ordinance requiring inhabitants to apply for................ 29
Hall on Seashores... 43
   As to title in salt marshes................................. 43
Hargrave's Tracts : As to Creeks of Ports 40
Harlem : First patent 1666.................................... 10
   Original boundaries 11
   Common lands vested in the community in trust for the town. 12
   Patent in 1667, restores name of New Harlem in place of Lancaster... 12
   Dongan patent in 1686, merely confirms previous grants......13, 15
   Land granted to the freeholders and inhabitants by these patents 15
   And constituted the town a corporation..................... 12

INDEX.

Ceased to exist as a corporation prior to 1819.................... 106
Act of the Legislature 1820, Ch. 115, appoints Trustees to sell
    Harlem Commons.. 13
Names of residents of at close of 1661............................ 28
Order of Director and Counsel to survey lands.................... 29
Territory of, granted to its freeholders by Gov. Nicolls as Agent
    of Duke of York... 30
Harlem Farm, first account of................................... 17
Harlem Creek, or Montagne's Kill : 1, 2, 19, 21, 27, 30, 31, 72, 74, 75,
    77, 79, 81, 82, 86, 87, 95, 102, 107, 112, 114, 118, 120, 121, 123,
    ....124, 128, 129
    The outlet of three fresh water streams......................... 107
    And Mill Pond, history of....................................... 74
    Not an arm of the Harlem River.................................. 74
    Granted to the freeholders and inhabitants of Harlem........76, 125
    Opinion of Murray Hoffman as to tittle.......................... 125
    The question of title never has been passed upon 125
    Not navigable in the legal sense................................ 128
    Divided by the Mill Dam 129
    Harlem Creeks : Not calculated to raise the presumption that
        they were public and navigable............................. 83
    Included in the Harlem Patents 85
    No limitation in the grants.................................... 85
    No part of the Harlem Creeks were granted to New York by the
        Dongan Charter 104
    Not navigable waters... 85
    Even if navigable, the title passed to the town of Harlem and
        its grantees 85
    Had not *caput portus* and were not arms of the sea............ 83
    Were in a wholly unpopulated country when the De Forest
        and Van Curler's grants were made 83
Harlem Canal... 113
Harlem Marshes : See Meadows of Harlem.
Harlem Mill Creek, History of.............................107, 124
    Crossed by Second avenue in 1837 126
    Presumption that it was not a public stream.................... 126
Harlem Patents : Interpreted..............................10, 127
    Copies of in Appendix C, constituted the freeholders and in-
        habitants a corporation 12
    And the common lands were vested in the corporation........... 14
    "Heirs," the word in grant refers to the estates held severally as
        individual property 15
Hoffman Estates of New York...................................... 92
    As to rights of discovery 4
Holroyd, J.: Opinion in Rex v. Montague.......................... 81
    Opinion in Vooght v. Winch (2 B. & A.)........................ ib.
Hop Garden, The 97
    Owned by Maria Vermilje, widow of John De La Montagne, Jr.   96

INDEX.   193

Appendix B.. 4
Houck : Navigable Rivers in England...................... 36
Hudde, Andries... 17
   Member of Van Twiller's Council....................... 17
   First Commissary of Wares............................. 19
   Obtained ground brief for the De Forest farm in 1638.. 17
   Deed to of first Harlem farm.......................... 17
Indians : Only temporary occupants of the soil........... 9
   Their title by occupation acknowledged both by Colonial and State Governments................................. 9
   Their title extinguished by Minuit, Director General in 1626... 9
Indian Deed : To De La Montagne of Rechawanes (Montagne's Point), and the meadows in the Bay of Hell Gate........ 89
Indian Titles.. 9
   To land, doctrine as to stated........................ 9
Indian Trails : The only roads........................... 20
Indian War : instigated by Gov. Kieft.................... 22
   Resulted in the desolation of all the farms in Harlem, begun in 1643, and continued until treaty of peace in 1645.. 22
Inhabitants of Harlem in 1661............................ 28
Jennings, ex parte....................................... 57
Johnson, Simon : Assignee of Elias Pipon, conveys the mill property to Benjamin Benson..................................... 111
Jus Postliminii.. 4
Kuyter, Jochem Peterson : One of the Schepens, and Schout.... 27
   Farm of, called " Zegendael "......................... 26
   Account of burning his house, and his murder by the Indians. 26
Kent, Chancellor : Commentaries, V. 3, p. 427, review of as to tidal streams.. 71
Kieft, William, Director General......................... 22
Lancaster : Early name for New Harlem.................... 12
Land ; Distribution of by Dutch Government............... 29
   Ground briefs disregarded............................. 29
   Division of Harlem common land........................ 92
Le Roy, Jacob : See Waldron Williams.
Littledale, J.: Opinion of in Rex v. Montague............ 81
Littoral owners, right of. See Tidal Creeks.
Lossing's Encyclopedia of U. S. History, right of discovery... 5
Lovelace, Governor, gives order to repair the Mill dam during De Lavall's absence... 108
Manhattan Island : Settlement of by the Dutch............ 4, 9
   Origin of land titles on.............................. 5
   Purchased from Indians................................ 9
Mansfield, Ld. : Opinion in Lynn v. Turner (1 Cowp. 86), in 1774... 45
   " The flowing and reflowing of the tide does not make a navigable river.".. 46
   The most recent statement of the law as to tidal streams when the constitution of the State of N. Y. was adopted.......... 55

INDEX.

Marshall, *Ch. J.*: Opinion in Johnson *v.* McIntosh (8 Wheaton, U. S. R.)... 5
   Right of discovery.. 5
McGown, Margaret : Lineal descendant of Johannes Benson....... 1
   The Montagne's Point farm.. 1
   The McGown marshes or meadows in the bay of Hell Gate, title stated (see Meadows of Harlem)................................. 85
McGown, Samson Benson : Deed to by Margaret McGown of part of the McGown Marshes... 103
Meadows : In Bay of Hellgate title approved........................ 89
   Described and classified.. 85
   Title to extinguished and reverted to Government............. 30
   Added to Montagne's Point farm................................. 1
   Continued under one title until it came to Margaret McGown in 1821... 1
Meadows of Harlem : Account of..................................... 87
   Included in the Harlem patents; a distinct formation of land; John Archer claims some in Harlem river, Govr. Nicolls' order in regard to same... 85
   Allotments of.. 88
   Highly prized by the owners of farm ; salt hay thought to be indispensable ; historical extracts.............................. 89
   Small section still extant.. 89
   Division creek in the McGowan meadows........................ 88
   Two distinct titles and part included in the first ground brief to Montague allotment to Dutch Church of part of meadows in the Bay of Hellgate.. 88
   Conveyed to Montagne by the Indians ; and by the town ; conveyed by Montagne to Bogert................................ 89
   Van Oblinus claims a small section of Bogert's meadows and claim sustained... 91
   Conveyed by Bogert to Johannes Benson....................... 95
   The McGown meadows defined as dry land..................... 103
   Title more than 200 years old.................................... 103
   Conveyed by Margaret McGown to Edward Sandford and Samson, Benson McGown... 103
   No doubt about the title until filled in......................... 103
   Not included in the Dongan Charter to New York.............. 104
   Opinion of Richard O'Gorman, corporation counsel, as to..... 105
   Conclusion as to the title.. 106
Merewcather Sgt.: Speech of in Attorney General *v.* Mayor of London, and Jerwoods reply thereto........................... 34
Mill Camp, the... 27
Montagne, De La, Johannes... 21
   Deed to must be construed according to the common law when given... 8
   Petition of Jacob Kipp and Wm. De La Montagne to Gov. and Council in New Netherland to establish a village............ 27

INDEX. 195

Montagne, De La, John, Jr.: Deed to, from Magistrates of Harlem
of Montagne's Point and meadows in Bay of Hell Gate and
effect of same... 30
Title carried to centre of creeks, see description................ 31
Interpretation of deeds to the De La Montagnes involves examination of law as to tidal creeks............................... 32
(See Tidal Creeks), the creeks or kills mentioned in these deeds
were not arms of the sea or of the East river................. 33
Not large enough to raise presumption that they were public
or navigable rivers.. 33
Ebb and flow of the tide in these streams cause the embarrass-
ment as to rights of Riparian owners........................... 33
This is largely owing to misapprehension of the law relating
thereto.. 33
Montagne's Flat and Point: Included in the first Harlem farm..... 1
Originally one farm... 1
Allotted to Isaac De Forest...................................... 17
Conveyed to Andries Hudde.. 17
Historical references to the farm................................ 17
The outlying lands... 20
Conveyed to Dr. Johannes La Montagne, counsellor of New
Netherland... 21
Desolated by the Indian War...................................... 22
Ordinance establishing the village of New Harlem................. 23
The Flat set over to the village and the title to the Point con-
firmed in John De La Montagne, Jr.............................. 30
For subsequent title see Meadows in the Bay of Hell Gate and
McGown Marshes.
Morgen: Two acres, distribution of meadows.................. 19, 24
Muscoota: Indian name for Harlem Plains........................... 1
Navigable streams (see Tidal Creeks): Not determined by ebb and
flow of tide... 45
Public navigation must be open and notorious................... ib.
New Harlem, village of: Founded in 1658.......................... 23
Establishment of, related by O. Callaghan, Brodhead & Riker,
Riker's account.. 23
Ordinance in regard to... 24
New Netherland: Seizure of by British forces...................... 2
Dutch relinquish title to... 3
Patent to the Duke of York..................................... 2, 4
Commission of Gov. Nicolls....................................... 2
Dutch and British Claims stated................................ 2, 8
New York: Constitution of 1777................................... 54
Grants by State of so far as relates to tidal waters has not
been changed.. 54
Was adopted ten years before De Jure Maris was published... 55
Nicolls, Richard, Governor: Advent of British fleet and forces
under, in New Amsterdam.. 2

INDEX.

Patents to Harlem granted in 1666–7, p. 10, and Appendix.
Order in regard to certain Harlem meadows.................... 85
O. Callaghan: Hist. of New Netherland extinguishment of Indian
    titles 10
Opinions: As to title of Samson Benson (son of Johannes) to Montagne's Point...99, 100
    On the Harlem Patents....................................... 10
    As to origin of the title to Manhattan Island................. 2, 8
    On deed of Town of Harlem to John De La Montagne, Senior,
      of Montagne's Point and Montagne's Flat................... 29
    On deed of Town of Harlem to John De La Montagne, Junior,
      of Montagne's Point and adjoining meadows................ 30
    On deed of Benjamin Benson to Samson Benson of Montagne's
      Point.. 103
    On deed of Benjamin Benson to Peter B. Benson, of the farm
      on northerly side of Harlem Creek, with the Mill stream,
      Mill, and Mill pond....................................... 114
    On deed of Benjamin L. Benson to Harriet M. Wiswell........ 123
    On title of Margaret McGown to the marshes in the Bay of
      Hell Gate... 102
    On title to Harlem Creek..................................... 81
    As to the navigability of the Harlem Creeks.................. 85
    Of Judge Murray Hoffmann as to title to Harlem Creek....... 125
    Of Richard O. Gorman, corporation counsel, that New York
      has no title to the McGown marshes...................... 106
    Of William C. Whitney, corporation counsel, as to the Harlem
      common lands, Appendix D, E and F....................... 106
Ordinance: Of Director-General and Council to found the Village
    of Harlem.. 24
    Directing inhabitants to take out ground briefs............... 29
Outlying lands: Access to....................................... 20
Oyster Bay: See Wadsworth, J.
Parker, *Ch. J.*: Opinion in Commonwealth *v.* Charlestown,
    1 Pick. Mass. R., 179.. 56
Patents (see Harlem): To the freeholders and inhabitants of Harlem, construed... 12
    Copies in full in Appendix C.
    Constituted the freeholders and inhabitants a corporation.... 12
    The common lands invested in them as joint tenants in trust
      for the town.. 15
    The second Nicolls patent a confirmation of the first.......... 13
    Peaceful Vale, or Vredendael................................. 10
    Montagne's farm.. 10
Peters' Reports: Martin *v.* Waddell............................. 5
Pipon, Elizabeth: Wife of Philip Pipon and daughter of James and
    Frances Carteret, inherits the Mill property................. 110
Pipon, Elias: Son of Elizabeth and Philip, inherits the Mill property,
    by way of entail.. 110

INDEX. 197

Assigns all his property to Simon Johnson and others	111
Johnson, surviving assignee, conveys the Mill property to Benjamin Benson	ib.
Point Rechawanes	89
Questions: As to beginning of titles on Manhattan Island	2
Arising out of Dutch Grants to be construed by common law	8
Rechawanes: Indian name for point of land lying between Harlem Creek and Creek at the south	1
Rex v. Montague (4 B. and C., 598): Examined	79
Riparian Owners: See Tidal Creeks.	
Roberts v. Baumgarten	72
Relating to Harlem Creek	ib.
Compared with Rex v. Montagne	79
Neither the Harlem Patents nor the Montagne Deeds in evidence in that case	77
Some facts in regard to Harlem Mill Creek overlooked in that decision	79
Court of Appeals decision in that case, how to be regarded	78
Has never decided that all tidal streams are public and navigable	79
Round Meadow	86
Salt Marshes: Account of	42, 43
Title to creeks in, is in the owners of, ebb and flow of the tide therein does not raise a presumption that they are *publici juris*	43
Highly prized by the farmers	44
Sandford, Edward: Deed to by Margaret McGown, of part of the McGown marshes	103
Savage, Ch. J.: Opinion in Rogers v. Jones (1 Wend., 238), as to lands under water at Oyster Bay	56
Schorrakin: See "Zegendal."	
Second Avenue: Established by law across Harlem Mill Creek in 1837	126
Proceedings for opening	ib.
Shaw, Ch. J: Opinion in Rowe v. Granite Bridge Co. (21 Pick., 344), as to ebb and flow of tide being test of a stream being public	66
Shores of the Sea: Defined	42
Stony Island	14
Stuyvesant, Governor: Allotment of lands	29
Establishes the Village of New Harlem on Swit's boundary and the Van Keulen tract, and part of Kuyter's land	23
Revokes the ground brief to Dr. John De La Montagne, of Montagne's flat, and confirms the title in Montagne's Point	29
Summary: As to Harlem Mill Creek and Mill Pond	128
"Successors:" Meaning of word in grant	15
Sutherland, J.: Opinion in Rogers v. Jones (1 Wend., 238), as to lands in Oyster Bay	56

INDEX.

Taney, *Ch. J.* : (Opinion in Martin *v.* Waddell, 16 Peters), right of dicovery 5
Tappan Indians : Bill of sale of Rechewanis Point to John De La Montagne 89
Tidal Creeks : Ebb and flow of tide not always the test of a stream being public 32
 There must be public use or navigation to raise such presumption 32
 Private navigation may exist in: theory that all tidal streams *prima facie, publici juris*, not sustained by English common law 32
 The treatise *De Jure Maris* responsible for that theory, but does not teach the doctrine 32
 The occasional use of small tidal streams for the passage of vessels does not of itself raise the presumption that they are public 33
 Private property in beds of tidal waters has existed to a large extent from remote periods of time 33
 Immemorial use the test 34, 43
 Legal presumption that a stream is navigable, when applicable . 38
 Littoral proprietors of, in tidal waters 33
 Lord Mansfield did not recognize the ebb and flow of the tide as the test 46
 There must be a public navigation to show that a small stream is public 46
 What is meant by a public navigation 46
 The King has not title as universal occupier of vacant lands .. 50
 Three kinds of rivers, tidal, that are navigable and not navigable, and inland rivers 50
 In England, few of the rivers in their natural conditions were navigable above the flow of the tide 52
 The title of the King to tidal waters a common law question .. 52
 The common law is the outgrowth of facts 52
 Common law doctrine as to rights of littoral and riprarian proprietors 52
 Navigable, what are *prima facie* 53
 Grants bordering on private streams, construction of 53
 If a small tidal stream has become of public use, the Court will not take judicial notice of the fact 53
 The Constitution of the State of New York was adopted ten years before *De Jure Maris* was published, and grants must be construed according to the law existing when they were made 54, 55
 Grants by the State of lands on tidal waters may pass title to the lands beyond high water mark 56
 The King's title extends only to those waters which are actually navigable 62

INDEX. 199

The books show few cases in which the title to the soil of salt water
    creeks has been involved... 62
Rivulets a distinguishing feature of Manhattan Island.......... 83
All of them filled in excepting two or three, emptying into the
    Harlem river... 84
The Harlem Patents having included all the creeks, the pre-
    sumption is that they were not public waters.................. 85
In grants of lands or private streams made by the Sovereign
    to a subject, the title extends to the thread of the stream
    unless otherwise expressed.. 53
Tide-way : The strip of land between ordinary high and low water
    mark... 76
The grant of Governor Dongan to the City of New York, of
    the tide-way, did not include the salt marshes nor the Harlem
    creeks... 76
Thurley, J.: Opinion in Elder v. Burras (6 Humph., Tenn., 366)... 60
Tourneur, Daniel... 14
Town Records of Harlem : Show grant of the Church Meadows in
    the Bay of Hell Gate, to John De La Montagne, in exchange
    for property. (See Appendix B.)................................... 49
Treaty of Westminster.. 3, 4
Treaty of Breda... 4
Trustees to sell the Harlem Commons................................. 92
Tyler on the Law of Boundaries : Rivers where the tide ebbs and
    flows belong to the public only in those parts which are
    navigable.. 53
Unappropriated Lands in Harlem all disposed of.................... 12
Van Curler Tract : Account of... 19
Van Curler, Jacob: First proprietor of Van Kenlen's Hook, known
    as Otter Spoor, or Otter Track................................... 1, 9
Van Kenlen's Hook... 1, 19
Van Oblinus, Joost claims a small section of the meadows in the
    Bay, from Bogert, and brings suit................................. 91
    Judgment in his favor, Appendix B.............................. 5
    His farm at Hoorn Hook, adjoining Montagne's, described... 91
Vercher's, or Hogg Island.. 14
Van Arsdale, Peter : Husband of Wilhelmina Benson.............. 120
Van Twiller, Wouter: Second Director-General of New Netherland 19
Van Schoonerwoert : See Bogert, John Louwe......................
Van Tievenhoven : Secretary of New Netherland.................. 26
Verplanck, Senator : Opinion in Canal Commissioners v. Kemps-
    hall (26 Wend., 404).. 54
Village of New Harlem : Founding of................................. 23
Vooght v. Winch (2 B. and A., 662)................................... 47
"Vredendal" : Montagne's farm on Harlem Flats..................
    The De Forest Farm.. 19
Woodworth, J.: Opinion in Rogers v. Jones (1 Wend., 238), as to
    lands under water at Oyster Bay.................................. 56

Wagon Road: To be built 25
Waldron, Resolved: Never owned Waldron farm.................... 94
Waldron, Samuel: Farm of, described 94
Waldron, William (son off Samuel): Came into possession of Waldron Farm in 1741, and set off part of it to his brother Benjamin, and another part to Jacob Le Roy 94
Waldron Farm: Country seats of Astor, Gracia, Prime and Rhinelander included in... 94
Walworth, Chr.: Common Law of England and not the Civil Law in force in New York.. 7
 Opinion of, in Childs v. Starr (4 Hill) 70
 In Canal Commissioners v. The People (17 Wend., 8)........... 6
Westminster: Treaty of, 1874 3
Whitney, William C.: Corporation Counsel, Opinion of, as to Title of the City of New York, Appendix D and E................... 106
Wey Schut: Boat used to bring hay from the meadows 86
Woodward, J.: Opinion in McManus v. Carmichael (2 Clarke's Cases, Sup. Ct., Iowa).. 60
 The tide a merely arbitrary test as to navigability and appropriation to public use .... ib.
Woolwych on Waters... 46
York, Duke of: Patent from Charles II............................... 4
 Commission to Nicolls 30
Yacht Rensselaerwick 17
Zegendal or Schorrakin: The farm of Jochene Peterson Kuyter, of 400 acres 26

www.ingramcontent.com/pod-product-compliance
Lightning Source LLC
Chambersburg PA
CBHW020858230426
43666CB00008B/1229